Writing a Watertight Thesis

Writing a Watertight Thesis

A Guide to Successful Structure and Defence

MIKE BOTTERY AND NIGEL WRIGHT

BLOOMSBURY ACADEMIC
LONDON • NEW YORK • OXFORD • NEW DELHI • SYDNEY

BLOOMSBURY ACADEMIC
Bloomsbury Publishing Plc
50 Bedford Square, London, WC1B 3DP, UK
1385 Broadway, New York, NY 10018, USA

BLOOMSBURY, BLOOMSBURY ACADEMIC and the Diana logo are trademarks
of Bloomsbury Publishing Plc

First published in Great Britain 2019

A catalogue record for this book is available from the British Library.

A catalog record for this book is available from the Library of Congress.

ISBN. HB: 978-1-3500-4695-5
PB: 978-1-3500-4694-8
ePDF: 978-1-3500-4698-6
eBook: 978-1-3500-4696-2

Typeset by Deanta Global Publishing Services, Chennai, India
Printed and bound in Great Britain

To find out more about our authors and books visit www.bloomsbury.com and
sign up for our newsletters.

CONTENTS

ACKNOWLEDGEMENTS

There are many people we would like to thank in helping us reflect upon our practice of supervision, in approaching the writing of this book, and in commenting upon various drafts as it developed.

First, we would like to thank all those students we have worked with over three decades, and from whom we have learnt so much about the practice of supervision.

Second, we would like to thank all those successful doctoral candidates from our own institution and from around the world who graciously agreed to the use of their experiences and their doctoral work to illustrate particular points throughout the book.

Third, we would like to thank the large number of colleagues from other institutions who have invited us to act as external examiners at their institution, and so expand our experience; and many of whom for also acting as external examiners for us.

Finally, we would like to thank those individuals who helped us specifically with the book, either by reading individual chapters or by engaging in discussion on the project: Julian Stern, Peter Gilroy, Elaine King, John Greenman, Mike Whitehouse, Tim Scott, and Clive Opie.

Introduction

Writing a doctoral thesis can be an arduous and confusing process, and particularly at the beginning, when students may understand that they need to produce a strong structure for the entire work, but may be unsure about how to do this in a clear, rational and convincing manner. This book demonstrates how to produce such a 'watertight' thesis – how to set up a thesis structure and how to maintain it throughout the doctoral journey. As the book explains, the key to such watertightness begins with the ability to work out what the main research question of the thesis is, and what are the sub-questions derived from it, the answers to which collectively answer this main one. If then you follow and structure this approach throughout your thesis, you can be confident that your examiners will find it extraordinarily difficult to fail your thesis on structural grounds.

Writing a Watertight Thesis illustrates this argument with examples of how theses can be made more watertight. In many cases the examples are ones taken from genuine theses. These were only used once permission had been granted by the authors, in terms of thesis content, our comments upon these theses, and the identification of the authors' identities. All of these theses are referenced at the back of the book. Other examples were created by us – with advice from individuals more specialized in these areas – to demonstrate how widely the approach taken can be adopted. The book also provides doctoral candidates with numerous exercises enabling them to do the same kinds of things within their own thesis.

Finally, we have taken the decision to not include detailed discussion of action research and grounded theory methodology approaches in this book. We still believe that the approach taken in this book is applicable to both: they both need to set up a thesis structure and maintain it throughout the doctoral journey, and they both need a main research question and sub-research questions, which collectively answer the main one. Nevertheless, discussion of the individual complexities of these two approaches would require a disproportionate amount of space in a relatively short book. In the circumstances, we recommend a number of more specifically focused books for those interested in taking these approaches (see Appendix 1).

Writing a Watertight Thesis will then provide greater clarity to the doctoral journey for many students: it will make the whole process more comprehensible and enjoyable, and crucially, it will make the entire thesis much easier to defend.

PART ONE

Moving in

In the first section of this book, key issues of structuring at the beginning of a thesis are examined. Chapter 1 begins this process by examining the need for, and the meaning of the term 'watertight'. Chapter 2 gives advice on developing the structure of a research proposal so that it works to your advantage in your application and if you get called for any interview. This proposal then is very likely the first structured conception of your thesis structure. Finally, Chapter 3 explores the early meetings you will have with your supervisors, and how such meetings can help in developing this doctoral structure, as your initial conceptions move into a more concerted framing of your thesis.

CHAPTER ONE

The need for a 'watertight' thesis

Introduction

A generation or two ago, it was fairly normal for doctoral students to arrive at a university and spend the first few months reading around a topic until at some time during the first year, they came to an understanding of what the thesis might consist. Whilst reading round a subject is an important early activity, students and supervisors alike now face new pressures. Students now have strong demands to finish on time. They may be paying for this study themselves, they may have a scholarship or funding body which expects completion within the allotted time period and they may have a family to support. Supervisors, irrespective of national location, want students to finish on time with a quality piece of work, which launches them along their chosen career path. They also tend to live with increased work pressures and external expectations of students completing on time. Both student and supervisor then have strong reasons for wanting to waste as little time as possible, to establish the focus of the thesis fairly early on in the study, how this can be framed to suit the specified length, and then developed during the period of study so that satisfactory data are gathered to provide the final answers in the concluding chapters.

Yet our joint experience of half a century of supervising and examining over 160 doctoral theses, with students from virtually every continent on the planet, and from a wide range of academic and professional backgrounds, is that lots of doctoral students still come to university with limited understanding of what to expect, what a good doctorate looks like, and how to spend their time on study most profitably. They can find it very difficult to understand what needs to be done at the beginning of their thesis, and particularly in terms of its overall structure. This book provides them with these understandings from the start, and in particular helps them establish their thesis structure in a convincing and clear way, so that they can maintain this through to the end of their programme. To do this, they need to produce a watertight thesis.

This book is written for students in the first place, but it also is likely to be useful for supervisors new to the task, and for those beginning to examine doctorates. To start, then, we want to explain how 'watertight' theses have major strengths that other theses may lack. We also need to reassure you that what is recommended is not just the parochial approach of a couple of UK academics but also applicable internationally.

So, what is a 'watertight' thesis?

A 'watertight' thesis is fundamentally one demonstrating such sound structural integrity that it is nearly impossible to demolish its main argument. It means that if your thesis is structured in this way, then an examiner will find it enormously difficult to fail it on structural grounds, a critical aspect of doctoral quality. The suggestion of needing to be 'watertight' is borrowed from shipbuilding, where the builders of river and sea-going vessels need at all costs to keep the water out, that is to ensure that the internal parts of the ship and the people on board, along with any cargo, remain dry and afloat. To do this, shipbuilders need to adhere to a number of principles. In particular, they need to ensure

- that the ship is properly designed;
- that the right materials are selected for its given purposes; and
- that there is such a synergy between design and materials in the ship's construction that no water can seep in.

These need to be tested, and not just before the ship puts out to sea. The building of the ship needs to be tested throughout a process which includes sea trials to ensure the ship's watertightness. If you look at Table 1.1, you'll see that the early stages of thesis construction are very similar. They should include determining the general area of research, designing appropriately focused key questions, stipulating the range of contextual information required and deciding on the appropriate thesis structure to generate the

TABLE 1.1 Stages for constructing the watertight ship and thesis

	Ship	Thesis
Design	Determining the kind of uses for which the ship will be used; the kinds of environments the ship will inhabit; designing appropriate internal and external physical structure to avoid leakages	Determining the general area of research, designing appropriately focused key questions, the range of contextual information required and the appropriate thesis structure to 'deliver' the answers
Materials	Appropriate materials selected to ensure watertightness, and the manner of application in building the ship	Determining the data that are needed to answer key questions, and the modes of investigation by which the data will be accessed and gathered
Construction	Good construction ensures that the synergy of design and materials guarantees watertightness	An appropriately structured thesis ensures synergy of questions, context, data and analysis, and provides defensible answers to critical questioning
Testing	Tested throughout the building process to ensure the ship's watertightness, before finally embarking on sea trials.	Tested in an iterative manner throughout the research process to ensure the creation of defensible answers by moving back to earlier stages for adjustment as necessary

answers. The 'materials' necessarily include determining the data that are needed to answer the key questions, and deciding on the modes of investigation by which the data will be accessed and collected. The actual construction of the research must be reflected by an appropriately structured thesis, which ensures the necessary synergy between questions, context, data and analysis, and thus provides defensible answers to critical questioning. When talking about testing, we avoid using the term 'finally', as this may suggest that this only needs doing at the end of the process: in fact, any thesis needs to be tested by initial questions and comments from your supervisors, and later on by means of formative assessments, where your work is scrutinized in critical detail. This provides the doctorate with the ability to move back and forth in its examination, and to adjust earlier stages as necessary.

Does 'watertightness' work for different kinds of doctoral studies?

The traditional way of gaining a doctorate has been to study for a PhD or a D Phil., the key output being a thesis of up to 100,000 words, examined by a number of examiners, some internal and some external to the university at which it is written. Many universities also conduct an oral examination of the candidate (a *viva voce*). Over recent years, however, doctorates have changed considerably and are now characterized by a paradoxical mixture of standardization and variety: the standardization of an increasing internationalization of similar regulations, accompanied by a greater marketized diversity of programmes. Universities have then broadened the choice of ways in which candidates can pursue doctoral research. In the process, a range of 'professional' doctorates has been developed, which can include taught and/or performance elements, aimed at meeting the needs of mid-career professionals, who may study on a part-time basis. These include the DBA (Doctor of Business Administration), DPsych (Doctor of Psychology), the EdD (Doctor of Education), and the D Prof (Professional Doctorate). All, however, still require a research-based thesis, though these tend to be shorter than those for a traditional PhD/DPhil.

In addition to PhDs and professional doctorates, there are also 'doctorates by publication'. For these, candidates are required, as part of their submission, to present a number of already published academic articles on a central topic in peer-refereed journals. Chapter 12 of this book deals with the writing of such articles. A crucial element here is the requirement to write a 'connective piece', normally of between 10,000 and 20,000 words, which shows how the published papers link together to generate a new and original contribution to disciplinary knowledge.

Whatever the format adopted, coherence and structure are universally required, and therefore the watertightness of the thesis is essential for them all. This is not to say that the demands on a student in these different formats do not vary. For example, any temptation to think that the shorter 'professional' thesis is in some way 'easier' than a PhD is in our view seriously misleading: it may be even more demanding in a shorter form to focus a main question down to a precise and researchable issue when there are less words to play with. Similarly, the articles chosen for a doctorate by publication are not necessarily written with a systematic doctorate in mind, and therefore the writing of the argument of any connecting piece will be at least as demanding as in a 'normal' doctorate. So, whatever the format undertaken, whether traditional, professional, or by published work, the concept of watertightness remains central to its achievement.

Does the watertight approach work for doctorates in different countries?

Over the last two to three decades, there has been a move towards the development and adoption of 'qualifications frameworks' worldwide. A report in 2013 for the ASEM Ministers' Conference indicated that 142 countries and territories were now involved in developing qualifications frameworks (Bjornavold, 2013). Initially many of these have been nationally based (National Qualifications Frameworks, or NQFs), but these have also been drawn together into regional qualifications frameworks (RQFs). The most prominent of these regional frameworks is probably the European Qualifications Framework (EQF, 2005), but there are others such as that of the Association of South East Asian Nations (ASEAN, 2007). These qualifications frameworks provide a series of descriptors for different levels of learning outcomes for school and post school education. Now there is a growing consensus about the nature of key aspects of the outcomes of doctoral level study. So the UK descriptors indicate the need for the following:

- The creation and interpretation of new knowledge, through original research or other advanced scholarship, of a quality to satisfy peer review, extend the forefront of the discipline, and merit publication.

- A systematic acquisition and understanding of a substantial body of knowledge which is at the forefront of an academic discipline or area of professional practice.

- The general ability to conceptualise, design and implement a project for the generation of new knowledge, applications or understanding at the forefront of the discipline, and to adjust the project design in the light of unforeseen problems.

- A detailed understanding of applicable techniques for research and advanced academic enquiry. (QAA, 2014)

The Hong Kong qualifications framework similarly asks the student to do the following:

- Demonstrate and work with a critical overview of a subject or discipline, including an evaluative understanding of principal theories and concepts, and of its broad relationships with other disciplines.

- Identify, conceptualize and offer original and creative insights into new, complex and abstract ideas and information.

- Deal with very complex and/or new issues and make informed judgements in the absence of complete or consistent data/information.

- Make a significant and original contribution to a specialized field of inquiry, or to broader interdisciplinary relationships. (hkqf. 2017)

And finally, the Canadian qualifications framework requires that:

- holders of the doctoral degree must have demonstrated a high degree of intellectual autonomy, an ability to conceptualize, design and implement projects for the generation of significant new knowledge and/or understanding, and an ability to create and interpret knowledge that extends the forefront of a discipline, usually through original research or creative activity. (Council of Ministers of Education, Canada, 2007)

Note, for example, how similar is the UK descriptor, which asks for an 'understanding of a substantial body of knowledge which is at the forefront of an academic discipline or area of professional practice' (QAA, 2014), compared to the Canadian one for 'the generation of significant new knowledge and/or understanding ... that extends the forefront of a Discipline' (Council of Ministers of Education Canada, 2007).

We can also see such commonality through the examination of a successful Czech doctorate by Michal Simane (2015), which demonstrates that similar criteria are recognized and adhered to elsewhere. The major research question of the thesis was the following:

What were the everyday and major challenges encountered in Czech minority schools in Usti nad Labem during the first Czech Republic, and how successfully were these challenges dealt with?

Michal recognized the need to ask questions about the context of his study by looking at the social, political and economic backgrounds during this period, to ask more specific questions about how these schools were set up and run, and how well they managed to cooperate with other non-Czech schools. He also recognized the need to ask questions about the best possible methods for examining the daily life and challenges of these schools. These led to his triangulated approach, which included archival resources, legislation, historical periodicals, period photographs and memoirs of students at these schools. His conclusions allowed him to produce new understandings for the region he explored. In terms of the UK criteria,

- He created new knowledge, through original research, which satisfied peer review, and which extended the forefront of his area of study discipline, parts of which were published.

- He systematically acquired and came to understand a body of contextual and focused knowledge which was unique and therefore at the forefront of his academic area.

- Using his triangulated approach, he demonstrated a detailed understanding of applicable techniques for his research, and thus was able to conceptualise, design and implement a project generating new knowledge and understanding in his area. (QAA, 2014)

Both the frameworks and the doctoral example above highlight the importance and centrality of appropriate questions, as it is these which orientate research from what is believed to be known into what is currently unknown, because at the end of the journey, one of the results will be the production or creation of insights and materials which were not known or recognized before the research was undertaken.

The main point of these different national examples then is to demonstrate that most doctoral studies are guided by similar qualification framework languages, and that our approach will then be helpful under most doctoral rubrics whether the research takes place in the UK, Hong Kong, Canada, the Czech Republic, or in most other countries.

Does 'watertightness' work for doctoral studies in different disciplines?

Most of the materials in this book are applicable to doctorates in all disciplines. This is largely because theses in different disciplines have many things in common, and therefore need to be watertight in the same kinds of way. The most important of these commonalities are as follows:

- they all need a description, explanation and justification of a central research question, which requires answering in the thesis;

- they all need a description and justification of a thesis structure which demonstrates how this central research question will be answered;

- they all need to explain and justify how the research makes an original contribution to the discipline;

- they all need to describe and critique the relevant literature(s) pertaining to their study;

- they all need to explain and justify the methods which will be used to gather data in order to answer their central question.

This book then shows the doctoral student how to develop a thesis structure providing a watertight way of answering a central research question. It shows not only how literature reviews are more than just reviews of appropriate literature, but also strategic explorations of thinking and research in their field to better frame and justify the originality of their research question. It also demonstrates how the selection of research methods in empirical theses, to appropriately answer the main research question, is also critical to thesis structuring. These issues, and their proper structuring into your thesis, will go a long way in making it defensible and watertight, whichever discipline you are working within.

Nevertheless, there are some differences between disciplines in their attitude to doctoral thought and practice, and they may affect the way in which structuring is approached. Disciplines can then differ in the content and structuring of theses in the following ways.

Using hypotheses rather than central research questions

Some disciplines, most notably scientific disciplines, talk in terms of 'hypotheses' rather than key research questions (Kerlinger, 1969, Bryman, 2015). They do this arguing that the scientific method is based upon the idea that one begins with a theory, extracts a prediction from that theory, and then finds the evidence to test whether that prediction is true or false. If the prediction is validated, then the theory is strengthened. If the prediction is falsified, the theory is invalidated. Whilst personally questioning the finality of any such invalidation (see Chalmers, 2005), the important point here is that such a thesis begins with a prediction rather than a question, and the prediction is then tested. Now, by seeking to either confirm or falsify hypotheses, this approach imposes restrictions on the type of answer one can gain; the hypothesis can only be either accepted or rejected. Some may then think that because predictions focus tightly and testably upon one aspect of a theory, it is then better to adopt an approach where more nuanced questions and answers are more possible. Questions, properly framed, can perform the same function; it depends, unsurprisingly, on the tightness and focus of the questions being asked. Take the fairly general prediction given by Cohen and Manion (1994, p. 18) that

> social class background determines academic achievement.

It is a simple matter to turn this into a key research question for a thesis – what will subsequently be called its Major Research Question (MRQ) – which then becomes the following:

> Does social class background determine academic achievement?

The prediction requires evidence to see if it is validated; the question similarly requires evidence for it to be answered. However, a question like this also admits the possibility of a range of 'answers' if it is phrased thus:

> To what extent does social class background determine academic achievement?

The reverse – going from question to prediction – is also possible. Here we take Simane's doctorate (2015) referred to earlier. Michal agreed that its MRQ was the following:

> What was the everyday life and the major challenges encountered in Czech minority schools in Usti nad Labem during the first Czech Republic, and how successfully were these challenges dealt with?

One hypothesis coming from this, requiring evidence for its validation or invalidation, would be the following:

> Everyday and major challenges encountered in Czech minority schools in Usti Nad Labem during the first Czech Republic were dealt with successfully.

Of the two approaches, we prefer the 'MRQ' approach, because, as noted above, the answers in this approach lend themselves to rather more nuanced answers than those using an 'hypothesis approach'. It may be the case, after all, that some challenges to the schools were dealt with very successfully, some only partially dealt with, and some never resolved. Being directed by a hypothesis into positive or negative conclusions may miss some of the subtlety and nuance encountered in life. Conclusions to theses should be determined more by the nature of the problem than by the nature of the method chosen. As the book progresses, a variety of examples will be used to show how the deconstruction of an MRQ as a way of structuring a thesis can work as well – or better – than 'hypothesis' approaches.

Different views of the status of knowledge

Some disciplines believe that because of the methods adopted, the data gained from a thesis can be viewed as 'objective', standing beyond the influence or interpretation of any personal views. This view contrasts with disciplines which believe that any 'knowledge' gained is necessarily much more 'subjective' than this, as it is gathered by fallible and selective human beings, irrespective of the methods adopted. In disciplines where data is viewed as more 'objective', discussion of epistemology is in practice likely to be more limited in the methodology chapter of a thesis than where greater subjectivity is accepted.

Different views of reality

Such views of the 'objective' status of 'knowledge' gained are ultimately based on – or convince people of – the existence of a single unitary 'reality', and that research therefore can help in providing a 'more accurate' picture of this one reality. Such a 'realist ontology' needs contrasting with other disciplines which tend to believe that, because of the status of knowledge they believe is possible, there are necessarily multiple views of any such reality, and therefore a more limited 'interpretivist' view of research is more appropriate (Denzin and Lincoln, 2000). These contrasting views are likely to affect the degree to which such issues of 'ontology' are represented in the methodology chapter of a thesis. Both of these issues – the status of epistemology and ontology – will be considered in more detail in later chapters of the book.

Differences in the importance of context

Given the above, it will not be surprising to find that disciplines can differ in the degree to which they believe that different 'contexts' – historical, cultural, or professional – can affect and impact on the nature of a research problem and the results gained. Where methods and results are seen as capable of being context-free, this may be an issue receiving little consideration in the content or structuring of the thesis. In virtually all disciplines, however, one context is nearly always important to the study, and that is the history of the research into the topic being investigated. Where contexts are seen as capable of impacting on methods and data, then a great deal more attention needs to be paid to them, particularly those theses involving studies of human beings, as they are likely to be affected by different personal, institutional, or cultural perspectives.

Differences in positionality

Unsurprisingly, then, theses can also differ in the degree to which they believe that a researcher's experience, views, attitudes, values and perceptions – their 'positionality' – can impact on the conduct of the study, and therefore on the results. Where a study is believed to be very largely immune to such effects, discussion of such issues of 'positionality' may be seen as largely unnecessary. Where, however, they are believed to 'frame' the way a problem is viewed, and therefore researched, such positionality is likely to be seen as needing considerable thought and discussion in the thesis.

The way in which disciplines may see doctoral work differently raises the question of whether discussion of positionality issues needs inclusion or exclusion in a thesis. We think that a book such as this, whilst being a practical aid to doctoral researchers, also needs to ask doctoral students to reflect upon these kinds of questions, because they go to the heart of the doctoral exercise, in particular, how human beings gain knowledge, and the extent to which they can have confidence in that knowledge. As with the thinking behind all good doctoral theses, students then need to think about why different positions are taken, whether they can be justified, how they would be justified, and whether attempts at such justification should be part of the structuring and argument of their own thesis.

Why not use an 'Aims and Objectives' approach?

Finally, an often-used approach to thesis writing and structuring has been to employ 'aims and objectives'. Whilst superficially attractive, we believe that there are a number of inherent weaknesses in it. The first problem is that of vagueness in stating the aims. Aims are usually the statement of fairly general intentions, and may refer to things like 'Investigating practice and policy in Texan laboratories' or 'Exploring mentoring in the Finnish police-force', and may then fail to state explicitly the central focus of the thesis. Much the same problem comes with objectives; they can all too easily become a wish list of a range of potentially tangential issues which the researcher would like to explore, rather than explicitly stating what is essential for the argument of the thesis.

This leads to the central concern with using an 'Aims and Objectives' approach: there is often no necessary and explicit logical connection between them, and it can then be really rather difficult to demonstrate how the one relates to the other. With an 'MRQ' approach – where aims are replaced by a major research question, and objectives are replaced by research sub-questions – the link is both logical and watertight. As will be described in detail in this book, the research sub-questions are devised through examining and extracting the significant elements from the 'major research question'. Not only are they then *derived* from the major research questions, but their actual number is determined by the significant elements within the major research question. And to add to this essential symbiosis, if the researcher looks at the research sub-questions, and comes to the conclusion that another is needed to fully explain what needs doing in the research, then the major research question will need adjusting to embrace this extra element. The major research question and the research sub-questions then are intimately and inextricably joined by the fact that the research sub-questions can only be derived from the major research question, and the major research question is devised from the essential elements of the research. There can then be no vagueness in the expression of the main research question, and there can then be no additional research sub-questions beyond those encapsulated by the major research question. The links are therefore logical, symbiotic and watertight. This, we think, gives the 'MRQ' approach distinct advantages over an 'Aims and Objectives' approach, and as we shall see, particularly when it comes to the structuring of the thesis.

So now, having completed the explanations and justifications for the approach, let's move to Chapter 2, where we examine one of the first demands for good structuring: when a candidate writes a research proposal to the university of their choice. So let's look at the best ways of structuring a doctoral proposal.

CHAPTER TWO

Structuring your proposal

This chapter is written primarily for students needing to write a doctoral proposal which will be read and evaluated by a team at a university. However, there are some, particularly those taking professional doctorates, who may have this task delayed until one or two years into their programme, because taught elements may constitute the first part of the course, and the research proposal will then be delayed, possibly becoming the final written assignment of this initial taught element. Some professional doctorate applicants may then wonder whether this chapter is relevant to them. We think there are a couple of reasons for thinking that it is. First, it is quite possible that students will be asked about initial thesis ideas even at any initial interview and acceptance stage, and it is always helpful to have some coherent ideas on thesis construction, even if the details are likely to change by the time the final focus of the thesis is decided upon. Perhaps more importantly, the next few pages can help students approaching the end of a taught element, as this chapter discusses and provides advice on the kinds of structural questions that any final assignment on a forthcoming thesis will need to include.

However, for the applicant trying to put together a coherent proposal, there are normally three major issues to deal with in the doctoral application process:

i   the completion of a formal application form;
ii the framing of a coherent research proposal; and
iii finally, in many cases an interview when the first two elements have been evaluated.

Whilst this chapter focuses on the framing and structuring of a coherent research proposal, it will also be invaluable for any subsequent interview, as the development of coherent structure in your proposal will be very useful in helping to deal with any questions asked there.

Now you may have consulted the website of your chosen university and identified academics working in your area of research, and they may even be advertising for doctoral students to carry out part of the work of a research project for which they have gained a grant. Whichever of these is the case, you need to ensure great clarity in your proposal because, if this is lacking, your chances of acceptance are greatly reduced.

Structuring and writing a good research proposal are like writing a doctorate, iterative processes, and you must expect to go through a number of drafts before you have a version good enough to submit. Whilst you may think that such processes are relatively straightforward, there is more to developing a watertight structure than you might think.

For a start, you will need to demonstrate that you have some interesting ideas, which may not yet be fully formed, but which, if you can draft them into a proposal displaying coherence, logical progression, good acquaintance with literature in the area, and some initial ideas about methodology, are likely to be viewed positively.

Now you may already have realized that your research proposal structure is in many ways a microcosm of what the structure of your eventual thesis might look like, and the following six sections will help you to devise the key sections for your proposal. They are the following:

a The introduction
b The key contexts
c The central concepts
d The evidence to be gained
e The methodological approach and the methods to be used
f The working title

Each will be discussed in turn, and you will be given help in writing a short piece on each before moving to the next. Together, they will help you arrive at a first full draft of your proposal. You will then encounter some exercises to help you develop this first draft, by making the structure clearer, and any implicit assumptions identified and questioned and then either removed or better incorporated into the proposal. There is more to structuring a proposal, then, than just writing sections and paragraphs. How you use language can demonstrate consistent structure in your thinking, or indeed, the lack of it.

So the following paragraphs outline the basics of a proposal structure, and you are invited to draft your first version along these lines using the six key subheadings outlined above.

The introduction

The introduction to your proposal needs to do four things in particular:

- it needs to describe your interest in the topic, issue or problem which needs researching;

- it should sketch out an outline of this problem;

- it should explain your background, and to what degree this may impact on the problem you propose to research – it then outlines your 'positionality';

- it should set out the structure for the rest of your proposal.

So, to begin with, write four paragraphs, amounting in total to no more than one side of A4 paper, which begin with the following:

a I am interested in the subject of_____because_____.

b The issue I see as needing investigation is_____ because_____.

c I am particularly well suited to researching this issue because_____.

d So in this proposal I will_____.

Do this on your computer now.

The key contexts

Your proposal will probably require clarification of the main context(s) which may impact on your research. Many contextual factors are cultural/geographical, such as 'in Mexico', or 'in Portugal'. However, they could also be historical: for example, 'in the fourteenth century' or 'in the 1980s'. There are many other forms of context – political, linguistic, religious or professional – and you should consider whether they need mentioning because of the impact they could have on your project.

If some are important, write – again in under one side of A4 – a section which begins:

a The key context(s) which need taking account of when researching this doctorate are … .

1 _____because_____.

and then possibly

2 _____because_____.

3 _____because_____.

Complete these before you move on.

The central concepts

In this section you present your thoughts about the concepts and literatures impacting on the topic you intend researching. No thesis or research proposal is a 'free floating' document. Even Isaac Newton said that 'if I have seen further, it is by standing on the shoulders of giants'. So you need to show that you have begun examining the research literature which already exists on the subject, and indicate the relationship between this literature and your proposal.

So again, in less than one side of A4, write a piece beginning with the following:

a The main literature relevant to my thesis proposal is_____.
And next

b Knowledge of this literature is important to my
     thesis because_____.

Do this before moving on to the next section. If you have to admit to yourself that you don't know this literature very well (or even not at all) then either you have some homework to do, or you need to seek another topic where you have better background understanding. If you have to do more homework, then it is not advisable to progress further until you have done this, as the literature you now read may change your ideas about the viability of your proposal.

The evidence to be gained

In a research proposal, any section on the kind of evidence you need to investigate is at this stage necessarily rather tentative, because subsequent discussions with your supervisors will likely suggest that different or additional evidence is needed. However, you can still indicate here the sort of evidence you think will be important to answer your research problem, and from where this may be obtained, and what, from your reading, you think can be done to generate its acceptable doctoral quality (through discussions of issues like validity, reliability, trustworthiness, etc.) (see Bryman, 2015 on this).

So again, in less than one side of A4, write a piece beginning with the following:

a The most useful evidence to gather for this project then
     would be_____because_____.
     And then

b I would try to ensure it is robust evidence by_____.

Methodology

This can be a confusing term for the beginner and will be discussed in considerably more detail in Chapter 8. But essentially 'methodology' is an overarching term asking for your reflections on the fundamental principles of research, on the selection of the appropriate techniques or approaches to investigate your research question, and a description and discussion of the practical application of these methods in your research. In your proposal, you should provide reasons for the kind of data that need gathering *before* you provide a description of what you think are the best processes and methods for gathering this data. In other words, describe your ends before you describe the means of achieving these ends.

One further warning: the UK descriptors for doctoral work state that this approach implies

> a detailed understanding of applicable techniques for research and advanced academic enquiry. (QAA, 2104)

Don't take this too literally. Your reader doesn't want to read a short book demonstrating that you have a comprehensive knowledge of possible research techniques. Instead, they want you to show them that you are able to *select* those approaches most useful for investigating your topic, and are able to give good reasons for this selection. So, in less than one side of A4, write a piece beginning with the following:

> The most appropriate methodological approach to adopt in investigating my topic is_____because_____.

> And within this general approach, the best methods to use are_____because_____.

Again, write this section up before moving on to the final section.

The working title

Now that you've written up all of this, read it through and reflect on whether it changes your initial thoughts on your proposed thesis. Then write in just one sentence, and in no more than two to three lines, a brief summary of what you want to investigate:

> In my thesis, I want to investigate_____.

Read this summary again, reflect on it and then write it as if it were a working title for your thesis. So if your summary amounted to

> In my thesis I want to investigate the changing role of auxiliary nurses on orthopaedic wards in selected hospitals in Givenchy, France,

your working title would very likely be

> the changing role of auxiliary nurses on orthopaedic wards in selected hospitals in Givenchy, France.

Place this at the head of your proposal. Having now produced the first draft of your proposal, save it on your computer as 'Research proposal, Draft 1'. This will enable you to distinguish it from subsequent versions, which you should correspondingly label as 'Research proposal, Draft 2' and so on, for as many drafts as you need to write. It is good practice to keep such a record of these drafts, and of your development as a writer. You may also come to the conclusion, as you move through drafts, that material omitted in a previous draft should now be re-incorporated. So keep these records for future reference. It is a practice you should also employ with the drafts of your thesis chapters when you get to them.

Redrafting

With draft proposal 1 now to hand, there follows a series of exercises to help you redraft and sharpen up your proposal document. Each section will have a 'probing question' for you to consider except Section 6, which describes an approach to systematically structure your proposal document. If you have a friend or family member who is interested in supporting your work (they don't have to be experts at this stage) you can often make good use of their help by talking with them about how you want to answer the 'probing' questions which follow. This is a kind of formative discussion, in which, consciously and unconsciously, you are constantly trying to provide greater clarity about your ideas.

Section 1: The introduction

Probing question: Is the main focus of the research clear?

Sometimes it's a good idea to send the first paragraph of your introduction to your friend before any meeting, so that they don't feel pressured, and so that they have time to reflect on what you have written. If this is not possible, then provide a coffee at the meeting, and read to them, or get them to read this first paragraph. Then ask them the following:

> From what you have heard or read, what do you think is the main focus of this research?

It may be that you have written about several issues, and they may pick out one which you didn't think was central. Discuss with them why they chose this aspect, and then discuss how you might adjust your text to make clearer what you want to focus upon. If you have several foci, you need to consider which is the key one (or ones), and what the role of others in the thesis should be, and whether some need removing altogether. Do this before you move on.

Exercise – Interrogating definitions, assumptions and relationships

Now – either with your friend or on your own – revisit the paragraphs in your introduction and examine them in the following three ways:

1 Underline or highlight any *key concepts or phrases* used. Note what you think each word or term means, and then see whether a dictionary or your friend agrees with you, and if not, why you have taken the emphasis you have. Reflect on what this might say about any implicit meanings you have assumed in your writing but haven't fully recognized.

2 Be aware of the danger of assuming that you already have a good idea of what your thesis is going to conclude. A thesis should be focused on exploring whether something is or is

not the case, not on confirming what you currently think about an issue. So if you currently think that your thesis is going to be about proving that

> GM foods are damaging to dogs' long-term health.

Redefine this concern into a question like

> To what extent is GM food damaging to dogs' long-term health?

However, *don't* then select only that evidence which proves your personal belief! Show by your selection that your thesis will examine both (or all) sides of an argument.

3 Finally, ask yourself what the *relationships* are between your key concepts or phrases. Do they all link up? Do certain concepts need dealing with before others? Are some essentially unconnected to your central intentions? Do you need to better link these, or do some need dispensing with completely?

Now return to Draft 1 of the introduction, and redraft and restructure any parts you think need changing after these reflections. Do this before you address the next section.

Section 2: The context

Probing question: Do you need to better identify the context (or contexts) impacting on your research?

As we've noted, whilst some applicants may feel that contexts are not important to their study, in most cases there is at least one context – the history of the research into the topic they are investigating – which will impact on their research. But other contexts may be highly important as well. Any topic involving human beings, for instance, is likely to be impacted by different personal, ethical, institutional or cultural perspectives. One particular thesis (Albuhairi, 2015) researched cooperative learning in Saudi Arabia, and its Islamic context had considerable impact on the development of this form of learning in its schools, in contrast to that in many Western countries. It is then essential to work out which context or contexts are the most important for a particular study, and to justify this selection to the reader.

Research contexts will frequently appear in the title of a final thesis, and there may be good reason why they should feature in the title of your research proposal. By so doing, they not only add to the structural integrity of a proposal, but may also add to its originality (Wellington, 2013, Guccione and Wellington, 2017), and also to a better appreciation of the fact that 'originality' can have many meanings, which should provide comfort to the student who thinks that they have to produce a thesis with the originality of an Einstein (see Philips and Pugh, 2010). Researching a subject in a new context is then likely to be a strong mark of originality.

Exercise: So, return to your draft title, read it again and ask yourself whether or not it would benefit from the inclusion of a context or contexts. If you think so, and can justify such inclusion, then adjust the title.

Now read the section on context again, and ask yourself if it is sufficiently focused. This is important because you do not want to be accused of over-claiming or excessively generalizing from your results. If, for example, your context is that of the use of Batesian mimicry by selected species of moths in countryside near Nairobi, Kenya, it would be over-claiming if you said your context was 'Mimicry by Kenyan moths', or even more problematic, 'Mimicry by African moths', because your statements of context (and the type of mimicry) help determine the degree of generalization you are justified in making from the results of your research.

You also need to make clear in your proposal that a particular context is accessible to you. So, for example, you might want to research 'The formulation of hostage negotiation tactics by senior police officers in Victoria, Australia'. However, unless you live there and are actively involved in such work, or have high-level contacts with those who can provide you with access to relevant individuals, any research by you is going to be extremely problematic. Once again, this helps you indicate your *positionality* in the proposal – 'where you are coming from' – and what access your present position might afford you – or what problems it might pose for you.

So, reflect on these issues, and now make any necessary changes before you go on to the next section.

Section 3: Ideas and concepts in the literature

Probing question: Does your proposal present a structured approach to the important ideas and concepts in the appropriate research literature?

As already argued, you need to show good acquaintance with relevant literature on the topic you wish to research. In itself, however, this is insufficient, as you also need to demonstrate that you can write about this in a structured and informed way. And whilst you won't be able to provide a comprehensive overview in this short piece, how you structure in outline what appear to you to be relevant important literature in your proposal will help those reading it develop an assessment of your doctoral potential.

There are a number of important aspects enabling you to better structure your literature section.

First, with *content*, avoid the temptation to list all the content you know. Whilst you certainly need to demonstrate that you know some of the key authors and researchers in the field, you need to do more than provide a catalogue of them. Guccione and Wellington (2017, p. 89) argue that there are a series of writing 'gears' that you need to go through. So begin with things like paraphrasing, summarizing and analysing materials. With respect to this literature, ask yourself the following:

- Which present similar interpretations?

- Which approach the topic in different ways, either conceptually or methodologically?

- Which are referred to by almost all writers in the area?

Then be *synthetic* with the material. Ask yourself things like the following:

- Is it possible to make meaningful groupings of them?

- If so, how you might classify these?

- What 'labels' could you use to do this? Would this, for instance, be in terms of actual content, or in how the research was conducted?

Then *evaluate* this literature. Ask yourself the following:

- Where are the gaps in what you have read?

- Why do you consider them gaps?

- Which are the more robust of the studies?

- Why are they the most robust?

- How might your proposed research not only fit in with, but more importantly, develop this literature?

Exercise: So, now examine the current version of this section in your proposal, and where appropriate ask yourself the following questions:

- Have I made clear the salient issues on my topic?

- Have I grouped together authors if they take a particular approach or view the central topic in a particular way?

- How might I usefully classify or label these groups?

- Have I suggested where there may be gaps in the literature so far?

- Have I identified which studies might be considered as seminal because most writers refer to them in some way or other?

- Have I evaluated the quality of the studies mentioned?

- Have I included very recent sources?

If you can entice your friend for another coffee after you have rewritten this section, remind them of what you want to investigate, and then see if you can explain to them why you see some pieces as particularly relevant to your study. When you have done this, get them to tell you whether they understand your logic, or whether they feel you are still presenting them with little more than a catalogue of authors and their writing.

Finally, reflect on your friend's comments, return to your draft and rewrite the relevant section. At the end of this exercise, you should find this section more meaningful, more reasoned and more structured.

Section 4: Evidence

Probing question: What evidence will you need to collect for your research?

In your proposal it's a good idea to indicate the kinds of data you think will be important as evidence in answering the main questions of your thesis. However, it's normally *not* a good idea to collect evidence before you begin your thesis proper, because you will have extended discussions with your supervisors later which may change the nature of the central questions you want to ask, and therefore the kind of evidence which needs gathering. However, at this stage you can still demonstrate that you have a logical mind: you can make it clear that if X is the problem, then Y is the kind of evidence which will probably be the most useful in illuminating or resolving X. So, consider what types of evidence you may need. Your evidence may be experimental in nature; it may be historical; it may be conceptual; it may take the form of surveys or explorations; it may be perceptions of an issue; or it could be literary, textual or visual data. You may also want to *triangulate* this evidence – to try to resolve an issue with different forms of evidence, gained in different ways.

Exercise:
So, now look at your draft and ask yourself the following:

> Have I described and justified the kinds of evidence I think I am going to need to answer my problem?

Read the draft again and alter or include statements which better describe and/or justify the sorts of evidence which you think you will need.

Section 5: Methodological

Probing question: Is there consistency in the underlying structure of my methodological thinking? What methods seem the most appropriate for acquiring the evidence for my research?

Consistency in the underlying structure

It has already been suggested that your proposal should contain a section in which you indicate the processes that you think, at this stage, will underpin the conduct of your proposed research. This is another aspect of structure where care is needed in the choice of words used. Many 'methodological' words also have 'everyday' uses, which can lead to them being handled loosely in a proposal. It is then important to examine the language used.

Exercise: Make a list of the verbs used in your proposal which convey what you are hoping to do and research, and compare them with the list in Box 2.1. How many are identical?

Some of these verbs imply the way in which you are thinking about 'reality' – your view on *ontology*. So words like 'discover' or 'examine' or 'find out' can suggest your belief in some form of objective reality existing independently of you and your research. An example of such a view would be a sentence like the following:

> In this research I intend to discover the most effective dose of a new drug for adolescents suffering from neck cancer.

Box 2.1: Verbs used in research proposals

Account for; analyse; ask; calculate; critique; demonstrate; discover; examine; experiment; explore; find out; illuminate; inquire; investigate; measure; model; perceive; test; understand

But it might also be used for a different kind of proposal:

> In this research I intend to discover the views of a sample of respondents about gender issues

Now whilst it may well be possible to determine in some objective sense the most effective dose of a drug, the use of the verb 'discover' when discussing views on gender issues is rather more problematic, as it may suggest that not only are such views permanent and perfectly articulated by the subjects, but that the researcher can fully understand what another person actually means, and that their own views won't colour such interpretation. If the topic of research involves examining the perceptions of others, it may well be better to use a word like 'explore' to investigate the views of a sample of respondents. This kind of verb, along with words like 'illuminate' or 'critique', suggests a different view of 'reality', one where people may perceive different versions of this reality (including the researcher's version!), and in which your research is interested in exploring.

Other verbs are more methodological in their implications. If you find you have used verbs like 'calculate', 'measure' or 'model', these tend to suggest an interest in quantification, with questions like 'what percentage ...', 'what proportion of ... '. And there are other terms, like 'experiment' or 'test', which might imply an interest in comparing groups or in testing hypotheses. So be careful in using phrases like 'wanting to measure respondents' 'views through a series of semi-structured interviews' because semi-structured interviewing is much more of a qualitative than a quantitative process (which *measure* seems to imply), and it may then be more appropriate here to use verbs like 'interview', 'ask' or 'inquire', where you are exploring or understanding a range of views.

So, be very careful about the implications of the verbs you use in your proposal and ask yourself if they are consistent with the methodological approach you are adopting and change any that are inconsistent with this. Structuring your language appropriately will suggest to the reader a greater degree of consistency in your thinking, and help prepare you before you go to interview.

Considering the most appropriate methods for acquiring the evidence for your research

Now it's already been suggested that in a thesis proposal, a description of the kind of evidence required to answer your research questions should come *prior* to consideration of methodological issues, because the nature of this evidence should drive the kinds of methods used, and not the other way round. So in this section of your proposal you should begin by restating and justifying what kind of evidence you are looking for to answer or clarify the central problem(s) of your thesis, and then describe which methods or research-gathering techniques are going to be the most appropriate. This applies to both empirical and non-empirical research: you need to be aware and justify in non-empirical work the kind of conceptual, ideological and philosophical methods/approaches you will be using to investigate the questions you are asking, just as in empirical work you need to be aware of and justify the research techniques you will use.

We've already asked you to complete paragraphs beginning

> The most appropriate methodological approach to adopt in investigating my topic is _____ because _____.

And

> Within this general approach, the best methods to use are _____ because _____.

But given the extra work you've now done on the earlier sections of your proposal, and the reflections you have made in rewriting these paragraphs, it now makes good sense to reflect upon what you've written in these paragraphs, and adjust them accordingly.

Section 6: From working title to preliminary main research question

You have now produced a full second draft of your research proposal, which includes a working title. There is one last and very important task to undertake. Stand back from your proposal document and try to see the big picture behind it. You are now in a much better position to ask:

What is the main question of this research proposal?

You have gradually adjusted the working title as you addressed the issue of context, and as you selected the appropriate verb or verbs for the title and main question. You have then been building up an initial working title from which an initial draft question for your study can be produced. So now take this working title and re-frame it as a question. Now answer the following question:

What is my major research question?

Finally, and to really impress your readers, you might also want not only to draft a main question for your study, but also to create a question which addresses the concepts/literatures/contexts, another for the methodological subsection and one for the evidence. These questions might then look something like the following:

What concepts/literatures/contexts do I need to address to inform my main question?

What evidence will I need to answer my main question?

What methods will be the most appropriate for gaining this evidence?

If you can provide answers to these questions, you should now have a very workable and well-structured proposal to debate and discuss at any future interview.

This chapter then has described an approach to systematically structure your research proposal. It is only the beginning of an iterative process, but it is a strong start. The next stage will be when you have been accepted by a university, and are now meeting your supervisors for the first time for more detailed discussions. It is to these – the early stages of considering thesis structure with your supervisors – that we now turn.

CHAPTER THREE

Structuring in the early stages

Introduction

The previous chapter explored the structuring of a doctoral research proposal. This chapter assumes that you now have a place to read for your doctorate, and have begun discussions with your supervisors. It therefore examines important structuring issues you will encounter early in your doctoral journey. The first section focuses on issues of structure likely to emerge from these initial discussions with your supervisors. Then we look at the importance of structuring your time on your project. Structural lessons to be learnt from reading successful doctoral theses are then examined. Finally, we examine the lessons that can be learnt from looking at the end of your doctoral journey, because knowing something about this can provide a great deal of help in ensuring a watertight thesis.

Initial discussions with your supervisors

Once you have completed a research proposal and been accepted for a doctoral degree, after initial formalities, you will meet with your supervisors. In these early discussions it is really important to clarify your research ideas. You should not assume that just because you have written a successful research proposal, you need not give further thought to the issues raised within it. On the contrary, further early discussions on the ideas in your proposal are crucial to a successful doctoral journey.

It is also worth noting that there is likely to be a different balance in discussions between a doctoral candidate who is researching a personally devised topic and one who is researching a topic which is part of a larger project funded by a research grant gained by their supervisors. The first kind of candidate is likely to have greater input into the framing and direction of their thesis at these initial stages than the second, who will be as much concerned with trying to understand their supervisors' larger project, and how their own research fits into this.

In both cases, however, the student needs to get into the habit of discussing their ideas, meeting challenges to them, and revising them. The process of formative discussion and evaluation is a key part of any doctoral journey, from any initial interview right through to a final thesis examination, and there are likely to be many such discussions during this process. Don't be upset if your supervisors criticize your ideas and problematize what you are proposing to do. A good supervisor will want to assume the role of not only supportive supervisor but also critical examiner, and therefore will want to critique your thesis from an examiner's standpoint. The aim then is not to belittle you or your ideas, but rather to help you to achieve greater clarity about key aspects and the overall direction of your research project.

Now when you meet your supervisors for the first time, several months may have passed since you wrote your proposal, so your ideas may have changed and developed during that time, and it is therefore a good idea to explain your ideas again without referring directly to the proposal, as what was written earlier may no longer be precisely what you now think the study should be concerned with. In so doing, you give yourself greater flexibility in explaining and further exploring your early thinking. Such discussion also gives your supervisors more understanding of what you think the doctorate is about, and how well this harmonizes with their ideas.

A first meeting can then feel quite muddled at times, and particularly so for those doctoral students who have not written a structured research proposal. They can then arrive at their university with no proper research question phrased, and with little more than a 'collection of writings': essays previously written around the topic, but which lack a central connecting focus. These essays may be very good pieces of academic work, but it is important that the student quickly realizes that to be employable in the thesis, there needs to be very careful discussions between student and supervisors on these very early in the process, on what are the central goals of the thesis, and how particular chapters of the thesis will contribute to these. Sometimes, such a 'collection of writings' can be turned into a genuine research focus. Sometimes, however, some or all of these early chapters cannot do this job, and then they may need to be set aside, or only certain ones utilized in the thesis.

Over these first few discussions, however, you should then become clearer about your topic, the precise questions you will research, and how you will develop a methodology to appropriately underpin this approach. Once again, at these early stages, there may be differences in degrees of clarity and development between different students: a doctorate funded within a research project will already be supported by some fairly robust ideas from supervisors taking a wider perspective on what is required; in more 'student-independent' studies, you and your supervisors may fairly quickly arrive at some initial ideas of what the overall structure of your thesis should look like, but you are likely to need rather more discussion and exploration.

Structuring your time

At the outset, the prospect of three or four years of full-time study, or longer if you are a part-time student, may seem plenty of time for the task ahead. Yet time will pass rapidly and may begin to slip through your hands if you have not structured it properly. And there are at least three different kinds of time management to think about here: academic time management, social time management, and supervisory time management.

Academic time management

In terms of *academic time management*, a lot of this is normally written into a student's work plan by supervisors and university.

Many universities have systematic and detailed literature on the number of meetings per year between students and supervisors, and particularly on their timing, their format, and how work will be assessed. Depending upon the country within which your doctorate is completed, you may also need to attend and pass training modules in research techniques and methods; these need to be planned for, as well as the assignments normally accompanying them. Moreover, it is now common practice at the end of each year for a university to schedule other supervisors to read some of your material, and to table discussions – almost formative vivas – with you and your supervisors about your progress. So a great deal is already likely to be structured into your work.

Yet you still need to do some serious structuring yourself. Doctorates vary in length and so it would be unhelpful if we discussed the time structuring of any particular length of study. Instead, we think it would be useful for you to think of dividing the length of both an empirical thesis and a non-empirical thesis into three periods. With an empirical thesis, as you will see from Table 3.1, we divide each of these periods into (i) the main tasks, (ii) the 'mopping up' tasks – those left over from the previous period, and (iii) the 'moving on' tasks – those which are central to the next period, but which you may do preliminary work on now. For a non-empirical thesis, the division is simpler but more fluid; the first period will likely be largely spent in reviewing the literatures to be covered, and the conceptual tools to be used; the second will probably be spent in the application of these tools to these literatures, before the third period is spent in coming to a series of conclusions concerning what this suggests for the major research question posed. We shall discuss this further a little later in the chapter.

In the first period of an empirical thesis, then, we suggest that much of your time will be taken up in such tasks as establishing the research focus and questions, determining the overall thesis structure, establishing relevant literature and documentary searches, and writing the first drafts of early chapters. However, as you move towards the end of this period, you will also likely have come to some fairly firm ideas on methodology, on the kind of evidence you need, and from whom and from where they are to be gained. So if this is an empirical thesis, you will increasingly be involved in writing the piloting of materials, organizing, gaining permission and access for things like interviews and questionnaires, some of

TABLE 3.1 The tasks of the different 'periods' of an empirical doctoral timeline

Tasks Periods	Main tasks	'Mopping up' tasks	'Moving on' tasks
1st period	(i) Establishing research focus and questions; (ii) structuring the thesis; (iii) establishing relevant literatures and documentary sources; (iv) writing these early chapters		(i) Establishing methodological concerns and writing chapters; (ii) writing and piloting investigative materials; (iii) organizing research arrangements
2nd period	(i) Conducting research, collecting any empirical data	(i) Writing final literature chapters; (ii) writing chapters on methods and methodology; (iii) writing and piloting final materials; (iv) adjusting research arrangements; redrafting earlier chapters	Beginning the description and analysis of early empirical data
3rd period	(i) Analysing and evaluating research results; (ii) coming to final thesis conclusions; (iii) writing these final chapters; (iv) final thesis redraft and submission	(i) Conducting final elements of research data gathering; (ii) redrafting earlier chapters	Preparing materials for publication

which will probably extend into your second 'period'. If it is a non-empirical thesis, your time will likely be spent more on determining and justifying the conceptual approach you will use.

As you move into your second period, if you have fieldwork to do, you move into this period's major task, that of conducting and collecting your data, which could involve much travel, much personal interaction, constant adjustments caused by unexpected changes to your schedules, and the formulation of your data through such things as extensive experimental work, the collation of questionnaire responses and the transcribing of taped interviews. At the same time, you still have some 'mopping up' work to do: you shouldn't forget that you may have methodology chapter(s) still to write, and probably should continue to redraft your earlier chapters, as your reading of the literature on your topic continues. And as you move towards your third period, you are beginning to determine the best means of organizing and presenting your material, and how best to write it up.

In your third 'period', you may be finishing off final data gathering, and the redrafting of earlier chapters. For empirical theses, this period is largely consumed by the need to analyse and evaluate this data, to put it into chapter forms and to begin drawing some conclusions and recommendations. Both empirical and non-empirical theses should be arriving at a real sense of the full form and thrust of the thesis argument – which may involve some adjustments to the initial chapters.

It is also the period when you are most likely to be tired, and most want to finish and can therefore be quite a dangerous time, as tiredness can lead to poor and under-drafted endings. But you need to maintain the standards you have set yourself so far when addressing this final structuring, and in attending to little but important jobs, such as referencing, appendices and page numbering.

All of these issues should involve discussion with your supervisors, and the building of timelines indicating the key milestones you intend to pass, and at which point in your programme you intend to meet them. And, of course, like much else in a thesis, the early drafts of such a timeline will require constant modification as new needs, new challenges and new opportunities arise. This is to be expected, and should not be a cause for great concern at first. Nevertheless, it is something you should keep a wary eye on, because if, for example, you have not completed literature chapters by the middle of the second period, or if you have not completed any data gathering by the middle of the third period, then these are likely to be issues you need to address with some urgency – though such issues should have been flagged by any tabled university meetings about your progress.

Non-empirical theses will also end up with the same kinds of issues – coping with tiredness, the pressures of submission on time, and maintaining quality throughout the thesis. As noted above, a non-empirical, like an empirical thesis will have a major focus and research questions accompanying it. Once again, literatures in the area under research will need discussing, and the collation of evidence and argument in exploring the central question will ultimately lead to a set of conclusions in answering it. Nor must we forget methodology here: a successful and highly praised theoretical thesis by Wong (2005) argued in a chapter entitled 'Methodological Considerations' that a philosophic hermeneutical method of investigation was essential for his investigation of spirituality in Hong Kong. This argues for a definition of 'methodology' which encompasses not only the research instruments but also the theoretical perspectives informing the investigation and collection of evidence. So the three time periods once again work well, if with a little more flexibility: the need to firm up the research focus and questions, the initial literature searches followed by more intensive exploration and discussion of new literature and evidence before the arrival at final conclusions and recommendations.

Social time management

Some problems in keeping to an appropriate timeline come from academic problems – researching and writing in a different language, writing critically rather than descriptively, or simply finding academic study tiring and challenging. However, many time delays occur because of social time management, which is best described as the other equally or more serious commitments people have – family responsibilities, crises in part-time or full-time working as the doctorate is pursued, and personal issues such as coping with disability, the determination of the best time for academic working, and the balancing of work with play so that both are possible.

Some social time management challenges may seem reasonably predictable and things which can be planned for. Yet, as the old joke goes, if you want to make God laugh, tell him your plans. The changes occasioned by the birth of a new baby may be planned for, but most parents who have had a first child will testify to how unpredictable life can become. Moreover, the management and scale of most challenges are almost always different from person to person, and many challenges – a sudden illness, the death of a loved one, new job demands or marital challenges – can be highly taxing and unexpected. There isn't and cannot be any simple set of solutions for these, but the comparison of a marathon runner with a sprinter is an idea to keep in mind. Marathon runners know there is a long way to go, they structure their race by determining how quickly they need to run over the length of the course, which parts will be particularly challenging, and they try to save some energy for the final run-in. This is no bad description of the doctoral candidate, who similarly needs to be aware of the length of their race, of the challenges they will face on the way, of the pace they need to maintain and of the spare capacity they need to try to create and reserve, not just for the end, but for dealing with the unexpected during their 'race'. Sustaining yourself and creating capacity for the unanticipated should then be essential elements of any structures built into the planning for your doctoral programme.

Supervisory time management

Finally, there is the relationship of you to your supervisors, and in particular, their management of you and your management of them (Philips and Pugh, 2010). Now Guccione and Wellington (2017) don't particularly like the term 'supervisor', concerned that it may suggest that the main function of such individuals is one of advising, overseeing and inspecting a student's work. Instead, they express a preference for the term 'coach' rather than supervisor, arguing that (p. 7)

> a good coach will minimize the advising they do, and instead ask questions that spark critical thinking.

We're not entirely sure about this. At the start of a programme, many students are likely to welcome a fair bit of advice and direction, and many, unsure as they may be about whether their work approaches doctoral level, will probably welcome critiques of their work which provide them with a better understanding of their progress, and how to improve. Moreover, supervisors increasingly work within a supervisory rubric outlined by their university and government, in which elements of advice and oversight will continue hand-in-hand right through to the end of the thesis. Nevertheless, Guccione and Wellington's sentiments seem substantially correct: the relationship between supervisor and student *should* change as a thesis progresses, and as the candidate grows to become much more the expert on their chosen topic. Here the role of supervisor will diminish, and the role of coach in the asking of questions to spark further critical thinking will increase. And if this transition in relationships doesn't occur, then both parties should be concerned.

Moreover, rules and requirements are not there simply to be followed – the student needs to understand the reasons behind formal structures and demands. You should then not simply accept advice, but where problematic ask the reasons behind it. Finally, it is not a good idea to have a problem and keep it to yourself: keep talking, discussing and reflecting with your supervisors – and with others who are in a similar position to yourself.

Over-directive and under-directive supervision

The above commentary should also make it clear that different people will hold different views on what is over-directive and under-directive supervision. For those who prefer a 'supervisor' rather than a 'coach', a coaching approach may be seen as under-directive. And for those who prefer a 'coach' rather than a 'supervisor', a supervisory approach may be seen as over-directive. Indeed, if one were to draw two axes, one for directive to non-directive supervisors, and the other for students preferring directive to non-directive supervisors, you would end up with four quadrants, but only two where there was a natural harmony between student and supervisor.

However, irrespective of the preferred type, it seems incontrovertible that the student should learn to – and want to – grow away from and beyond the coach or supervisor. In the end, such views may only be resolved by the development of good relationships. Unless, of course, worst case situations happen, and a 'coach' really refuses to provide any advice, and only asks questions at the start of the process; or a 'supervisor' really refuses to be less directive as the thesis progresses. In that case, a potential disintegration of the relationships would seem in need of intervention by someone external and perhaps more senior in the university hierarchy – and most universities now have the mechanisms to handle such disintegration between the parties involved.

In knowing what questions need asking

However, perhaps the most difficult problem for any new student is not in the asking of questions, but in not knowing what questions to ask. We suggest three major ways of dealing with this: talking to your supervisors, talking to successful candidates and exploring successful theses.

1 *Talk to your supervisors* Supervisors should be seen as a highly valuable resource. Not only have they almost certainly gained a doctorate themselves, and so know success from the inside, but they very likely will have supervised successful doctorates of varying quality. They will know that it is highly unusual for a thesis to fail completely, but they will also know that there is a range of judgements that can be made on thesis quality, and what extra work may be needed before a thesis is acceptable. It is therefore a very good idea to ask them their thoughts on such issues. They will likely draw on personal experience, cite particular examples, as well as refer to the doctoral rubric used in their university, all of which constitute useful background information. As these are only beginning conversations, you can and should develop them as your thesis, your understanding and your relationships develop.

2 *Talk to successful doctoral candidates* A further gentle way to begin is by talking to others who have completed doctorates, and ask them to reflect upon the issues that they have faced. Some issues they raise you may have expected, but talk a little longer on the ones that surprise you. If you come to really understand such 'surprises', you can better prepare for them. By so doing, you are in effect moving to the end of the doctoral journey, and thereby gaining a better perspective on the road you will be taking, and the tasks you will need to tackle. The lessons learnt from what really

matters at the end of your doctorate can then beneficially influence the early structuring of your thesis.

3 *Explore successful theses* The third way of knowing the right questions to ask is to look at the lessons learnt from completed theses. If you are engaged in early literature searches, your supervisors will almost certainly suggest that you read some completed theses in your area, and these will provide you with examples of overviews and syntheses you are also going to consult and read. And whilst each successful thesis makes a different contribution to knowledge in its chosen area, there are a number of things they all have to do which can provide helpful lessons for new researchers. Three in particular can aid your understanding of structure.

(i) *Examine some thesis abstracts* A good thesis abstract should give you a strong sense of the thesis structure. The abstract is the short summary at the beginning of the thesis, and is particularly helpful to readers and examiners wanting to gain a sense of what the thesis is about, and how it is structured. It should give a sense of the context, the key content presented, the methodology employed and the size and nature of the sample from which the data were gathered, as well as a final summary of what the key findings and outcomes are. All of this is normally required in around 400–500 words.

Some abstracts do this job very well, some rather less so. It can then be very useful to read a number of abstracts from theses in your field of study. After reading them, give each a score out of ten on how well they convey to you a sense of the thesis structure, and reflect on why you awarded the marks you did. Think about what aspects of your better examples would help you to better convey the thesis structure in your own abstract.

(ii) *Examine the introductory chapters of some theses* Another important structural device can be the introductory chapter of a thesis. You will see in the following chapters how important and valuable we think a well-organized introductory chapter can be. In many ways this chapter is an expansion of the abstract, helping the reader to better understand the 'thesis architecture'. To do this well, an introductory chapter should present the following:

a An overall description of the focus of the thesis, and the key questions addressed;

b A clear rationale for the purpose of each chapter in contributing to this thesis focus;

c A structured résumé of the key elements of each of the chapters;

d Explanations for why chapters are located in the thesis in the order in which they are presented.

Once again, the new candidate can learn how helpful introductory chapters can be through reading a number of such chapters. If you then return to the theses containing the abstract examples, we suggest you to now read their introductory chapters, and score them on the above criteria. The better ones will demonstrate well how the thesis has been structured, and should provide you with pointers on how to improve your own approach to this chapter.

(iii) *Look for structural devices throughout the thesis* Particularly helpful here for the reader is the provision of summaries at the end of each chapter, and careful introductions to the next, so that the way in which the thesis chapters build together to answer the main thesis issue is made explicit.

(iv) *Talk to successful doctoral candidates again* When you've gone through the previous four exercises, go back to your successful doctoral candidates, and now have a more informed discussion with them about the issues you now realize are very important.

Finally: Thinking about your examiners and the end of the doctoral journey

As we will argue throughout this book, it is helpful for most doctoral candidates to think of this doctoral journey as being similar to a train journey, and much more preferable than a mystery tour. Thinking of the doctoral journey as a train journey helps inject clarity and logic into the doctoral structure, which is better not only for the development of your writing but also for your examiners' understanding of the thesis, and they are critical to its success, as ultimately they make the final judgements on the quality of your thesis, and helping them better understand what you are doing will be essential.

So, as an introduction to thinking about your examiners, consider the following question: *What kinds of practices are likely to please them?*

The reason for the question may seem obvious: if you do things that your examiners approve of, you are more likely to get your doctorate. But to do well at this answer, you need to know a little bit about what examiners approve of. Yet your first reaction may simply be to say: how should I know? There is, of course, much that you currently do not know, and will only learn as you progress. However, your past experience with assignments, combined with the fact that your examiners are rational if busy human beings, should suggest to you that there are a number of things you probably already know which should be practised and structured into your thesis from the very start.

Exercise: Now before you read the suggestions below, make a list of your own ideas of what practices will please an examiner. Reflect on the things you have learnt so far about what makes a good essay or chapter, and what things your markers liked about them. Whilst it is often said you learn most from your mistakes, in fact you can learn a great deal from the things you do well. If you are a teacher or lecturer yourself, ask the following: what do *I* like to see in a good essay? So now make a list and save it on your computer.

Our own list would include the following:

- Adopt a critical rather than a descriptive approach to any review of literature in your area.

- Avoid repetition, wandering off the point or simply listing all the things you've read.

- Develop a writing approach which is clear, logical, structured and easy to read.

- Justify any assertions you make by providing evidence and appropriate references.

- Avoid phrases like 'It is clear ...', 'It is obvious that ...', 'It is well known that ... '.

- Spend time before writing working out what you want to argue, and how you will structure the piece to best express this.

- Before you hand in any written piece, draft and redraft it, so that what you hand in is the best that you can do at that moment in time.

Of course, as you write new sections of your thesis, you will become progressively more expert in the skills, the structuring and the expectations of these, and so will understand even better what examiners are looking for. Indeed, examiners' expectations are something discussed throughout this book, and will be the main focus of Chapter 10. So, as with your understanding of the argument of your thesis, if you can begin your thesis with some understanding of what your examiners want to read, you can progressively build and improve this.

    You have now taken time to consider the initial stages of moving into and structuring your thesis. You're ready to begin the process of structuring your research proper. So you now are ready to move to the structuring of a key aspect of your thesis, your major research question.

PART TWO

Moving through

CHAPTER FOUR

Focusing on the major research question

Introduction

The previous chapters looked at the kind of challenges and tasks that a doctoral candidate will probably face both before they arrive at university and when they first arrive. But it won't be long before the main doctoral tasks have to be tackled, and perhaps the most important one many newly arrived students need to deal with will be in getting their Major Research Question (MRQ) right. This does not need to be completed in its final form at the outset of your thesis journey: indeed we argue that 'the dance' of the MRQ and its attendant Research Sub-Questions (RSQs) is an iterative process, where each is changed by the insights gained from developing the other. This 'dance' is a frequent feature of doctoral work, as many doctoral students find that their well-planned methods encounter unforeseen problems in the literature investigations and in the collection and analysis of the research data, leading to necessary but unforeseen modifications.

Now, we have already talked about the structuring of your research proposal, and some of the advice in this chapter overlaps with that, but here we take the discussion much further. This chapter then examines the process of identifying the MRQ of a thesis, a critical starting point for your doctoral journey. As already noted, whilst you may well need adjustments to both the MRQ and the

RSQs, it is important that you have working versions of these from the early days of study, which you can modify in an iterative and flexible manner as your thesis develops.

What is the area of interest?

The purpose of your MRQ is to distil into one question what the thesis is seeking to answer. If properly posed and answered, it provides an essential focus from which you can create a robust framework for a successful thesis. We suggest that virtually all theses need these key distilled questions, but the process of arriving at them is likely to be highly individual, and dependent upon the background and interests of the student and the topic they wish to study.

However, before the MRQ is decided upon, it is important to drill down to an understanding of what the general area of interest really is. To provide you with some idea of how personal such journeys can be, here are stories of how two successful doctoral candidates went through a process of defining their general area of interest, before finally coming to their MRQs.

Sharron Wilkinson (2017) was an experienced prison educator who felt that effective prison education was hindered by policies which seemed to bounce between punitive and reformist aims with almost every change of government, and by an increasingly market-driven approach to the provision of such services. An initial concern lay in that Sharron's personal disenchantment with current policies on prison education might lead to the framing of a thesis question that attempted to provide proof for her own feelings about this situation. This seemed a dangerous road to take, as such an approach might lead Sharron into producing an MRQ, accompanying literature and research data, which simply reinforced such beliefs. Sharron and her supervisors therefore spent some time discussing this problem, and it was during one of these discussions that it was noted that there were interesting links between the 'wicked/tame' theory of Rittel and Webber (1973) and the manner in which the practice of prison educators seemed to be steered by current policies. Rittel and Webber had argued that despite living in a complex, 'wicked' world, there was a strong tendency to adopt rather simple, 'tame' approaches to problems, when more 'wicked' approaches were needed for such complex endeavours. Sharron quickly warmed to the idea, read extensively on this topic and began to adjust her focus to examining how and why government reforms had placed heavy pressures on the work of prison educators. This could then be described as a general interest in looking at

> the use of wicked theory to investigate whether policy pressures were leading to tame rather than wicked approaches to prison education.

Jeff Buckles's (2015) concerns about the environmental damage that humanity was inflicting on the planet were reflected in his early writing and discussions on this topic, and it became increasingly clear that he was as interested in the arguments to be found in the theoretical, ideological and global issues underpinning threats to environmental stability, as he was in his initial idea, of looking at how institutions were dealing with these issues. Indeed, as discussion went on, he felt the need to develop further his expertise in the theoretical issues, before he looked at any needed changes to institutional practices. So an initially empirically focused study changed to a more theoretical concern which examined the following:

> The philosophical and theoretical issues underpinning ecological sustainability, and how society needs to change to create a more sustainable world.

A first exercise

You're now ready to begin translating these examples into a personal focus for your own study. So under the title 'General Area of Research Interest', please write the following sentences onto your computer or in your research notebook:

> I have worked/researched in the area of_____for some considerable time;

> I'm really interested in one part of this area, which might be called_____.

I have noted that there is a question or problem in this area which I can't find the answer to in the academic literature, or which doesn't seem to be sufficiently covered to my satisfaction.

That question/problem is_____.

I'm really interested in answering this question because_____.

Some thoughts on your statements

Now, you don't *have* to be working or researching in an area to be able to research in that area. However, it can really help if you are, because you will know the background, the practices and possibly good contacts with whom to discuss this issue further. If you don't work or research in that area, then your supervisor will almost certainly want to ask you questions like the following:

● How much of the literature of this area have you read and understood? Tell me about some of the major writers and debates in this area;

● Is this an interest that you think you can sustain relentlessly for a number of years? A thesis is a marathon, not a sprint;

● How will you know when you don't know things about the area, things you should know about before you research in the area?

If you can't answer these questions, then you need to be honest with yourself and reflect upon whether you need to do one or some of the following:

a   Talk with others who are knowledgeable in the area about what they see as the key issues in the area;

b   Read more of the literature, the writers and the debates in the area of research you are considering;

c   Talk with trusted others who know you well and who will tell you *not* what you want to hear, but honestly about the likelihood of your staying the course if you were to pursue this area of study for a number of years.

If you find that you really aren't motivated by reading more in this area, or that some of the replies you get from friends and colleagues are quite negative (or simply aren't very positive), then you probably need to think again about this area of study.

One final point: you may have more than one area of interest or question; don't worry about this at this stage; go through the same procedures for all of them as above. The process of further discussion and reflection will very likely make it clear which is the one to pursue.

Coming to the Major Research Question: Taking your time and owning it

Now a simple but important point is not to rush this process. Give yourself – and your supervisors – time to discuss, debate and pass ideas around concerning the initial area of research. Tell them what you are interested in, discuss its possibilities with them and listen and try to respond to any issues they raise. In these dialogues with your supervisors, be happy if they lead at times in this early stage, but ensure that you voice your ideas and thoughts and that initial ideas are critiqued.

So, unless you are on a scholarship where the MRQ was largely decided before you applied for the doctorate (because it was one particular aspect of a larger funded research project, or has been stipulated by your sponsor), ensure that the MRQ expresses what *you* want to do, and is not derived simply from other people's authority, interest or enthusiasm. Now you may feel that the authority and expertise of your supervisors means that they should lead the way on deciding what the MRQ is about, simply because they know more about structuring a doctorate than you do. However, it is much better for you to be fully involved in conversations about its identification than to end up studying a problem defined by others. You need to be motivated to succeed in your study, and it is much more likely that you will approach this with enthusiasm, and keep going the extra mile, if you have what may be called a 'research itch': in other words, an issue of such intrinsic interest to you that you will want to find out the answer or the reason for it, simply because it fascinates you. Of course, we do assume that even if the

MRQ has already been defined by the research team who gained the funding for your scholarship, you are applying to them because you are really interested in this area, and not just because there is funding available!

Now whilst you may feel at the beginning of this process that you are the junior partner, this is a position that should change. Although you may feel at the outset that your supervisors have much more experience than you, your study should develop such that you should at some stage take over its leadership. At the end of the complete process, it will be *your* doctorate, not your supervisors', and you will be examined on its quality, and receive the credit – or the blame – for it. So very early on, commit yourself to listening to others, but accepting and embracing the fact that the ultimate responsibility for the doctorate is yours.

It is then really important that in most non-scholarship doctorates you arrive at an MRQ which expresses what *you* want to do and is not derived simply from others' authority, or research interests. Ensure that when you discuss the MRQ, you feel the 'research itch' mentioned above. You need to be genuinely excited about finding the answer to your question, though, as many doctoral students coming to the end of their study realize 'the answer' they gain may only be an initial answer in what turns out to be a preliminary study, with the doctoral findings suggesting that deeper more interesting things now need investigating.

A second exercise

Having answered these questions about the appropriateness of your chosen field of study as well as you can, again reflect on what you think currently is your major area of interest. Then, in no more than one sentence, write this down on your computer, or in your notebook:

My major area of research interest currently is_____.

Now read what you have written. Ask yourself: *Why have I written this down as my major area of interest?* Write down your reason(s) below your statement:

My major area of research interest is currently_____ because_____.

Below are a number of reasons you might have given. Which are the closest to the reasons you have provided? You can tick more than one, and add others. It is a good idea to rank them in order of importance. Your supervisor will be interested and probably want to discuss your reasons and rankings with you:

a My sponsor has determined that this is the area I should work in.

b My supervisor(s) has determined that this is the focus I should work in to contribute to a larger research project.

c This is what I'm really interested in doing.

d This is what my supervisor(s) think I should do.

e This is what I wrote when I applied.

f I thought the university would like the idea.

g Any other reason(s).

Now reflect upon your reason(s). Whilst all probably have some credibility, somewhere in your list should be included your personal interest in this area. It's important that you have the internal motivation to keep going for at least three years, and to enjoy this journey, and if you lack personal interest, your doctorate could become little more than a slog. This then starts the job of finalizing your MRQ. But you still have a little more to do.

Moving from your area of interest to your MRQ

Let's briefly return to Sharron and Jeff's areas of interest, to see how the transition from a general area of interest to their MRQs took place.

You will probably remember that Sharron's area of interest had become one of examining linkages between wicked theory and prison education policies, and particularly in whether policy pressures were leading to tame rather than wicked approaches to prison education. This area of interest was then turned into a question. The transition to Sharron's MRQ lay in her realization that wicked theory could act as a highly original investigative tool in coming to conclusions on this. In wanting to know what managers and prison educators themselves felt about the kinds of policies implemented, and the impact of such policies, the following MRQ was devised:

> What are the perceptions of two key stakeholder groups on the impact of tame and wicked approaches to prison education?

You may also remember that Jeff's area of interest lay initially in an empirical study looking at the institutional role in promoting global sustainability, but this had developed into a focus on the theoretical and ideological challenges acting on sustainability, and how such information might lead to the conceptualization of a new 'social imaginary'. Jeff's MRQ then became the following:

> What are the implications of developing a new social imaginary, brought about by the challenges to be faced in the twenty-first century?

So the reflections and discussions you have had on your area of interest should lead into a more tightly focused question – the MRQ. Importantly, then, don't leave this as a *statement* of a focused area of interest: make sure that you turn it into a *question which needs answering*, because this becomes the question that your thesis is trying to answer.

Now let's see if you can put this into practice with your own study.

A third exercise

On your computer or notebook, write down once more the following:

> My major area of interest is_____.

Now reflecting on what you really want to investigate in a focused way, complete the following phrase:

> So I want to ask_____.

And this, therefore, is your major research question.

Try to make this a reasonably short and lucid form of words – not more than one sentence long and not more than two to three lines long.

Now with a friend, or supervisor, discuss what you have written down and explore with them what this implies in terms of the following:

- Does this question really excite me? Does it give me a research itch?

- What kinds of contacts do I need in order to be able to research this question?

- What kind of literatures will I need to research to answer this question?

- What would seem to be the most appropriate research methods to investigate this issue, and why?

As you ask these questions and respond to them, try to understand and phrase better what you want to do, and so continue to adjust your MRQ to accommodate your emerging insights.

When you've done this, when you're happy with what you have arrived at, write down the draft of the MRQ you have now arrived at:

My MRQ is currently (date): _____.

Remember, the MRQ will probably need adjusting, expanding and rephrasing in an iterative manner for some time yet. This may happen throughout the first few months of your study, and perhaps longer than that. Further, as you develop your RSQs, and as you write individual chapters, this may lead to minor 'tweaks' in the phraseology needed to properly express your MRQ. This is perfectly normal, and might even be something you want to document in your thesis. After all, your examiners are not just interested in your findings, your claims and your conclusions, they are also interested in seeing how you developed as a researcher, to what extent you reflected upon the research process as you engaged with it and how much you were able to adjust to meet the questions and sometimes unexpected challenges that this process threw up for you. Whilst much of this never appears in published papers, most pieces of research go through such a reflexive and iterative process. And honesty in personal reflexivity is a key component of becoming a better researcher.

Creating a thesis title from the MRQ

Some readers may be wondering why the thesis title hasn't been mentioned so far and when it should be created. We've already provided advice on how to form one when writing a doctoral proposal, but many students will probably recognize by this stage that they have moved some way past this initial title. We suggest that the time for the formulation of your first full draft thesis title is now – when you have a workable MRQ with which you are comfortable. Finding the answers to your MRQ is the activity which drives the thesis, and so the thesis title is to a very large extent a statement of this focus. The thesis title commands the attention of the reader by being the first thing they read, but it is the MRQ which really drives the thesis work.

So the thesis title needs to reflect the concern of the MRQ. Now don't be afraid of being slightly boring, and don't try to be too clever. Whilst you need to be original and appealing with the titles of most fiction and non-fiction books, because they have to appeal to a public who need to be persuaded to part with their money, you are not trying to sell your thesis. Its title has a different task, which was captured very well in a UK television advert for household paint, which suggested that the appeal of the product lay in that it did precisely what it said on the tin. And this is your task: to describe as well as you can what the thesis does.

That being the case, we suggest that an acceptable title can have one of a number of variations:

A first variation is for the thesis title and the MRQ to be the same thing. This is clearly the simplest and most straightforward approach, and your university and examiners may not mind if the title is a question (but check the university regulations here). After all, they will read your title and then look to see if this is what is described and discussed in your abstract, and if this is what is answered in the RSQs, the chapters and in the overall thesis. So it's a straightforward way of dealing with this issue. An example of this would be the following:

> How does office architecture affect the personal wellbeing of long-term occupants?

A second variation uses the MRQ but then creates a title by dividing elements of the MRQ into two halves. An example here would be the following:

> Time and ethical concerns: Harry Harlow, maternal deprivation and animal rights.

A third and final variation would be one where you kept the essence of your MRQ, but provided a little more embellishment on the question within a thesis title which also becomes a statement.

> Swimming Against the Tide? The Challenges of Staging Modern Opera in Non-Metropolitan Contexts

A fourth exercise: Creating titles

So let's try creating some new thesis titles from MRQs.

Here are two more MRQs: Can you derive appropriate titles from them?

1   What were perceptions of Charles II's view of monarchy by members of his court?

   You could simply keep this MRQ as the title, but can you now

   (i)   Create a title as a statement for this highly similar to the MRQ:_____

   Perhaps: *The perceptions of Charles II's view of monarchy by members of his court*

   (ii)   Create a similar but more extended title: _____

   Perhaps: *The changing face of the monarchy under Charles II: Experiences and perceptions of members of his court*

2   Here's a second MRQ for you:

What role did climate change play in the extinction of Denisovan man?

Again, you can simply keep this MRQ as the title, but can you also create a title as a statement highly similar to the MRQ; this then becomes (rather boringly):

The role of climate change in the extinction of Denisovan man

(iii)   Create a similar but more extended title here: _____.

Perhaps: *Too variable a climate? An examination of the extinction causes of Denisovan man.*

A fifth exercise: Creating your own title

So now let's perform the same exercise with your own thesis. To begin, please write down, on your computer or notebook, your MRQ once more:

We've suggested that you have a choice here: (i) You can leave your MRQ as your title; (ii) you can turn your question into the statement of that question; or (iii) you can create a similar but slightly more embellished title. Write down all three variations:

The title as the major research question: _____

The title as a statement of the major research question: _____

The title as a similar but more extended title: _____

Now discuss all of these with your supervisors or a friend, and decide which seems most preferable. When you've come to a decision, make sure you can justify the choice.

Some final thoughts: Introducing the RSQs and the dance between the MRQ and the RSQs

Hopefully, by this stage, you have a form of your MRQ (as well as a Thesis Title) with which to work. If the MRQ is sufficiently well constructed, and if answered satisfactorily, it will go a long way in gaining you your doctorate. We can't say 'And if answered satisfactorily, it will guarantee the success of your thesis', because a thesis can be failed for a number of other reasons. If the reading of the area has been very poor, if the thesis is very poorly presented, or if it's plagiarized, then in all these cases a thesis can be failed, and this will have nothing to do with the quality of the MRQ or the structuring of answers to it. But we assume that these kinds of mistakes will not be made. So now, begin to work out how you derive the answer (or rather *the answers*) to your MRQ.

Now the crucial link between the Major Research Question and the Research Sub-Questions is that the MRQ is built up from a number of these smaller RSQs, and therefore the MRQ is answered by deconstructing it into these RSQs. So, if you have a strong and well-justified MRQ, and if you can provide adequate answers to all of the RSQs you deconstruct from the MRQ, then together these answers to your RSQs will provide a robust, defensible and watertight set of answers to the MRQ. As we've said earlier, like your MRQ, your RSQs begin as initial draft questions, and throughout the thesis process, and in reflecting on how they answer specific parts of the MRQ, they may well be modified. Of course, if this happens, they will also modify the MRQ. This is an essential 'dance' between them, though whilst they may change during the dance, we would still expect them, given a continued focus of interest until the end, to be reasonably similar to how they looked at the start of this dance.

So with a strong draft of your MRQ now down on paper and firmly in your mind, it's time to discuss how you derive your RSQs. We're ready to move to the next chapter.

CHAPTER FIVE

Creating your research sub-questions

Introduction

You have now managed a crucial task: the development of a workable Major Research Question (MRQ) for your thesis. Creating a main question and answering it satisfactorily will go a long way in gaining you your doctorate, because if your examiners accept that this is a valid question to drive a doctoral thesis, then answering it is an essential part of a successful thesis resolution.

Of course, and as importantly, you need to know how to go about answering your MRQ. This is where extracting the main elements out of the MRQ comes in, and from there you will be ready to construct your Research Sub-Questions. So let's take an example of this process, and then apply it to your own MRQ.

Moving from a general area of interest to a major research question, and then to its deconstructed elements

To demonstrate this process, we'll use the example of a UK student, Mike O'Dea (O'Dea, 2011), who completed doctoral studies in the use of computers. His general area of interest for his thesis was concerned with the educational use of computer gaming, and could be phrased as:

Developing educational computer games to enhance procedural and conceptual knowledge.

Ultimately, his MRQ became:

What are the key elements of a successful educational computer game designed to enhance the understanding of procedural and conceptual knowledge?

Now if you scrutinize this MRQ, you will see that there are a number of different elements of which it is comprised, and which require different forms of investigation.

Exercise: So now examine this MRQ closely, and ask yourself: What are the elements you think need separating out within this MRQ? At this stage, don't worry about being too precise, or of getting them in the right order. Just methodically work through the MRQ and extract all the elements which seem distinct from what else is said.

Now write them down on your computer, or in your notebook.

Interestingly, Mike, who wasn't our doctoral student, didn't extract the elements in this way when he wrote his thesis, but when we asked him to use our approach a number of years after he gained his doctorate, he suggested that from the MRQ

What are the key elements of a successful educational computer game designed to enhance the understanding of procedural and conceptual knowledge?

The key elements would need to be:

1 *The key features of educational computer games:* this is needed in order to provide an overview of what such games need to actually do, and how they do this.

2 *Designing successful computer games:* this is needed because the term 'successful' needs defining, and there may be many lessons to be learnt by examining what makes an educational game successful.

3 *Enhancing procedural and conceptual knowledge*: this is needed because defining and discussing these two forms of knowledge are central to understanding what a successful game needs to do.

4 *Ascertaining if learning has been enhanced*: this is needed because discussion of such measurement is essential to the meaning of the term 'successful'.

5 *The key features of the computer game contributing to this enhancement*: this is needed because it is the part of the question that helps us better understand the way that success is achieved.

6 *The kinds of methods to be used in investigating these issues*: this is needed because we need to be able to justify the best methods for investigating these issues.

Compare the elements you deduced for Mike's MRQ with his own deconstruction: do they differ? If so, how? Were any differences purely ones of phrasing elements, or did they go deeper and differ in actual meaning? If you have differently phrased elements, this isn't necessarily a problem; if you can justify what you have written, you may simply be phrasing the problem in a different way.

Now these elements clearly require further investigation. To be research sub-*questions*, they need to be further refined, not only into questions, but into questions which better express what needs investigation, and which, combined together, fully answer the MRQ. Now we already know that six elements should change into six Research Sub-Questions (RSQs), so let's do this translation.

Element 1 The key features of educational computer games
Now becomes
RSQ1: What are the key features of a successful educational computer games?

Element 2 Designing successful educational computer games
Now becomes
RSQ2: How can you design an effective educational computer game to improve procedural and conceptual knowledge?

Element 3 Enhancing procedural and conceptual knowledge
Now becomes
RSQ3: How can you define procedural and conceptual knowledge?

Element 4 Ascertaining if learning has been enhanced
Now becomes
RSQ4: How do you ascertain if procedural and conceptual knowledge has been enhanced by the use of an educational computer game?

Element 5 The key features contributing to this enhancement
Now becomes
RSQ5: If so, what are the key features of the educational computer games that contribute to this enhancement?

Element 6 The kinds of methods to be used in investigating these issues
Now becomes
RSQ6: What potential methods for investigating the MRQ seem appropriate?

Deriving the elements from your own MRQ

It's time now to derive the elements from your own Major Research Question. It normally helps if you can work with a colleague on this, but it is quite possible to do it alone. Write down your MRQ on your computer or notepad once more:

Now remembering how Mike's MRQ was deconstructed, see if you can divide your MRQ into different elements. Can you identify different foci, different issues, what you see as all the distinct features of your MRQ?

The number of elements will vary with different MRQs. Some MRQs only have four elements, some have five, and some have six; it is also quite possible that, as your thesis develops, you may separate out two RSQs from an original one; or you may combine two initial RSQs into just the one.

These elements will very likely consist of (i) relevant literatures, background materials or contexts you need to research; (ii) data you need to collect and (iii) the methods you need to employ to collect the data.

To cover these three areas in a doctoral thesis, you almost certainly need at least four elements: we'd be very surprised if you didn't need to research more than one relevant contextual or literature concern. So if you find, after your initial attempt, that you have less than four elements, see whether some of these are actually one or two elements fused together. But your MRQ is also unlikely to possess more than six or seven elements in total, so if you have more than this, see whether there is any repetition in the elements and if some can be fused together. However, there is no absolute rule here: each thesis will have its own construction of an MRQ, and its own deconstruction into RSQs.

So once more, read your MRQ, and try to identify the key elements.

Now go back to the MRQ, and referring to your elements, tick off each one referred to in the MRQ. If after you've done this, you've got parts of the MRQ which are still not covered, then you've got at least one more element to include. If however, you have got an element but no part of the MRQ left, then you have a choice: if you conclude that this element is not essential to what you need to do, then you can simply leave it out. On the other hand, if you think it is essential, then you need to revise the MRQ to incorporate it. But if you do need to revise the MRQ, then perform this exercise one more time, because the inclusion of an extra part to an MRQ can alter its full meaning and purpose.

Creating your own RSQs

It's now time to create your own Research Sub-Questions. So once again write down your MRQ.

You've already got your own list of elements derived from your MRQ.

So write them down again.

You now need to turn them into questions – your research sub-questions. So on your computer or in your notebook once more, take each element and turn it into a question – an RSQ. As you do this, write underneath each RSQ the reason for needing it.

You are now really beginning to structure your thesis, but before we go further, it's useful to once more raise a question we have touched on several times already: Does the MRQ generate the RSQs, or do the RSQs create the MRQ? This book has suggested that the process normally begins with the articulation of a general area of research interest, which then leads to the creation of an MRQ, but it is also clear that as you work through the RSQs, they may well affect the phraseology, structuring and even focus of your MRQ. In other words, this is an iterative process, not a simple linear movement, and you will almost certainly need to adjust, expand and rephrase your RSQs, as you fully develop them. Your RSQs then are unlikely to be fully or properly formed at the first attempt, and they will very likely change as you try to ensure that they fully encompass what you want the MRQ to ask.

Grouping research sub-questions

Now we've discussed literature reviews/background/context chapters, methodology chapters and data chapters, and it makes sense to align your RSQs with these chapters, rather than leave them without any order.

So once again, reflect upon the different RSQs which derived from Mike's MRQ:

RSQ1: What are the key features of successful educational computer games?

RSQ2: How can you define procedural and conceptual knowledge?

RSQ3: How can you design an effective educational computer game to improve procedural and conceptual knowledge?

RSQ4: How do you ascertain if procedural and conceptual knowledge has been enhanced by the use of an educational computer game?

RSQ5: If so, what are the key features of the educational computer games that contribute to this enhancement?

RSQ6: Which potential methods for investigating the MRQ seem appropriate?

Now, can you identify which of these RSQs are answered through

- literature reviews/background/context (LR)?
- the justification of methodology (JM)?
- the empirical research (ER)?

Read each one, and write either LR, JM or ER next to each RSQ. If possible, discuss your RSQs with a colleague to see whether they agree with you, and whether you can fine-tune the meanings of these elements. Not only does this give each RSQ greater precision; it also very likely gives you a more focused chapter title to address. For example, changing a chapter title from 'The Taiwanese context' to 'What are the Effects of the Taiwanese Context on Government Noise Pollution Strategies' or 'The Effects of the Taiwanese Context on Government Noise Pollution Strategies' gives you a much stronger chapter title to address, one that helps direct both your reading for the chapter and the writing of it.

So let's look at the probable answers to which kinds of chapters fit Mike's RSQs.

Answer:

- What are the key features of successful educational computer games? *Literature review and empirical research*

- How can you define procedural and conceptual knowledge? *Literature review*

- How can you design an effective educational computer game to improve procedural and conceptual knowledge? *Literature review and empirical research*

- How do you ascertain if procedural and conceptual knowledge has been enhanced by the use of an educational computer game? *Empirical research*

- If so, what are the key features of the educational computer games that contribute to this enhancement? *Literature review and empirical research*

- What potential methods for investigating the MRQ seem appropriate? *Justification of methodology*

You will have noted from this exercise that you can draw on different kinds of evidence to answer a single RSQ. Thus, part of the identification of the challenges to the development of the preliminary factors came about through:

  i Mike's literature review in this area

And part came through

  ii The data gained from his empirical research.

But also note that the literature review only gave Mike general findings. The data he gained during his empirical research made a significant contribution to the existing literature, and because his data was original, it added a new perspective to this literature. So when you come to the end of your thesis and attempt to fully answer the MRQ, you should discuss the similarities and differences between what the existing academic literature says about your questions and what new insights have been gained through the analysis of your own data.

Grouping the RSQs in an empirical thesis

We've already suggested that an empirical thesis almost always needs three kinds of sub-research questions:

  i RSQs derived from the literature/context/conceptual issues in the area of study (your literature review questions).

  ii An RSQ which justifies the methods you intend to employ (a methodology justification question).

  iii RSQs derived from your empirical research (empirical research questions).

So, given this, can you

  a identify the literature/context/conceptual Research Questions?

  b phrase the Methodology Justification Question (re-read the deconstructions of Mike's MRQ; very few Methodology Justification Questions differ much from this)?

  c identify the Empirical Research Questions?

Remember, some questions will require answers from your Literature *and* some from your empirical research. Write them down on your computer or in your notebook.

Now, in an empirical thesis, the Literature reviews usually come before the justification of the methodology, which normally comes before the empirical research. So to help you gain a better sense of your thesis structure, reorder your RSQs, with the Literature Research Questions coming first, the Methodology Justification Question coming next and the Empirical Research Questions coming last. Write them down on your computer or in your notebook now.

So now, let's pull all of this together and arrive at the first complete draft of your MRQ and RSQs.

Write the MRQ down in one line, and your RSQs, in the correct order, underneath it.

MRQ:

RSQs:

Grouping the RSQs in a non-empirical thesis

Whilst a non-empirical thesis hasn't got quite the same elements as an empirical thesis, it will have an MRQ as the driver of the thesis, and from this MRQ, RSQs can be similarly deconstructed and grouped. Take, for example, the case of the already mentioned thesis by Wong (2005). He did not use our procedures, but his thesis is a good example of the implicit use of our structure. Thus his thesis title was

> A conceptual investigation into spirituality and conditions for education in spirituality, with application to the case of Hong Kong

Given this title, he agreed that the following MRQ could then be derived:

> What are the current conditions, and future prospects, for an education in 'spirituality' in Hong Kong?

Further, in discussion with him on his chapter titles, he agreed that they reflect a deconstruction of his title/MRQ into the chapters necessary to answer it, which mirror appropriate RSQs. Thus

Chapter 1: Introduction and overview

Chapter 2: Methodological considerations

Both of these chapters are underpinned by an RSQ: *What methodology is most suitable for this thesis?*

However, Chapter 3: The Concept of spirituality is underpinned by a different RSQ: *What is the nature of 'spirituality'?*

Chapter 4: Conditions for Education in Spirituality is underpinned by a further RSQ: *What conditions are necessary for an education in spirituality?*

Chapter 5: Spirituality in traditional Chinese culture is underpinned by an RSQ: *How is spirituality expression and cultivated in traditional Chinese culture?*

Chapter 6: The Spiritual condition of Hong Kong and its Education is underpinned by the RSQ: *What is the current spiritual condition of Hong Kong and its education?*

Chapter 7: Possibility for education in Spirituality in Hong Kong is underpinned by the RSQ: *What is the current spiritual condition of Hong Kong and its education?*

Chapter 8: Conclusions and Recommendations

So Wong stated the problem to be investigated first, introduced his hermeneutical methodology next, moved to examine a number of literatures, before finally coming to concluding chapters on the spiritual condition of Hong Kong and the possibility of its improvement. He began, then, with title and chapters, but systematically if implicitly, worked through an appropriate MRQ and RSQs. The structure of this non-empirical thesis then follows much the same lines as the empirical theses examined above. One final word: non-empirical theses are quite as diverse as empirical ones, and the student will need to discuss with their supervisors the nuances of different approaches within their discipline.

Just one more time ...

So, well done! Take a breath, make yourself a drink, do something different for a few minutes. Then, when you've done some or all of these, return to the first full draft of your MRQ and RSQs, and ask yourself two questions:

a Do I still think that these RSQs, when added together, answer the full scope of the MRQ?

b Does the MRQ need expanding or changing to incorporate the scope of all of the RSQs?

As already noted a number of times, any changes will be part of an iterative process, as you move between the MRQ and the RSQs, adjusting both until you are happy with the balance between them.

When you think you are happy with what you have done, when you are confident that you now know what you are doing, you're ready for the final exercise of this chapter – the Café Questions.

The Café Question exercise: A formative viva

We've talked quite a bit about getting to a certain point in the initial stages of structuring your thesis, and now we want to suggest one way of gently testing yourself. We call it the Café question exercise. It is based upon the notion that one of the best ways to find out if someone really understands their thesis is for them to try and explain it to someone else. We imagined a situation where a candidate had just left a meeting with their supervisors, was feeling confident about their thesis, and went for a coffee, and began a conversation with someone they had not met previously, who asked them what they were doing. They replied that they were at the early stages of a doctorate, and this led to the other person asking them what precisely they were investigating. Explaining to someone in this manner was then based upon an old lecturing joke which states the following:

The first time you give a lecture, 25% of the students know what you're talking about;

The second time you give the lecture, 50% of the students know what you're talking about;

And the third time you give the lecture, **you** know what you're talking about.

It's surprising how much you can learn about what you really mean by trying to explain it to other people.

Now you can do this exercise with just one person, but it's also a good idea to find several people, and even better if these people are at a similar stage of their doctorate to you. We've run this exercise with classes of doctoral students, and invariably it is an enjoyable and profitable exercise. So you can do this with just one other person, or, and a little bit harder but probably more profitable, in groups of three or four. You are all in the same boat: you take turns in being the questioner and the respondent, and as the respondent, you are asked, and you need to answer in no more than thirty seconds, and without any notes, the following simple question:

What is your thesis about?

We hope that you try to answer this by referring to your MRQ (but it's surprising how some don't!). Now, if when describing what your thesis is about, you find yourself adjusting your MRQ as you talk, then reflect on the changes you are making, and why you are making them. Tell your questioner(s) what you have done, and don't be afraid to discuss this with them: after all, this isn't a competitive game in which they are trying to catch you out. On the contrary, their role is to help you to better explain what you want to research, and why you want to research this, just as shortly you will be asking them what their thesis is about, and trying to help them to better phrase their reply. When you are reasonably satisfied with your response, then write the MRQ in the new way, and continue with the exercise until you are sufficiently happy with it to feel that you don't need to make any more adjustments at this moment in time.

If, initially, you really struggle, and you don't manage to describe your thesis succinctly, don't worry: discuss with your questioner(s) why you think you are having problems, and then take your time to write the MRQ in a manner better describing what you really want to say, and repeat the exercise until you are happier with what you are saying. You may not get this completely right first time round, but you will notice continued improvement.

So, go through the full exercise a number of times with different people. After each exercise, if necessary, critique your MRQ, and adjust it in the light of the discussions. At the end of the session – or sessions – you should have an MRQ you can comfortably articulate.

In many ways, then, you have gone through, in a fairly non-stressful way, a small element of a formative viva, and your understanding of the thesis will be all the better for that.

Then, finally, introduce the RSQs ...

We think it's very likely that you've now got a strong understanding of the core of your thesis. If you agree, you should go one stage further, and let your questioner(s) ask you questions from the following list:

- What conceptual issues/literature areas/contexts will you need to investigate to answer your MRQ?

- Why do you need the conceptual issues/literature areas/contexts you have described and which are the most important?

- What kind of data will you need to collect to answer your MRQ?

- Why do you need the specific kinds of data you are going to collect?

- What do you think are the best ways of investigating these issues?

- Why do you think the ways you want to investigate your issues are the best ways?

If you haven't got someone to do this with you, simply write each of these down on separate cards, shuffle them and answer them in the order in which they are turned over. If you struggle with answers, then reflect on why you are struggling, and try to answer them again.

With or without a colleague, in answering these questions, you are describing and justifying what you are doing. In the process, you are beginning to move beyond a pure focus on the MRQ and its RSQs, and are beginning to ask some more substantive questions about the structure of your thesis, and the linking of the MRQ and the RSQs to the chapter structure of the thesis. It is to this vital exercise – linking the MRQ and RSQs to the chapter structure – that we now turn.

CHAPTER SIX

Linking the research sub-questions to the thesis chapters

Introduction

By now, you should have a fairly robust Major Research Question (MRQ), and derived from it some strong Research Sub-Questions (RSQs). But you may still be a little puzzled. You may be reasonably confident that you have a strong question upon which to base your thesis, and you may be comfortable with the questions you have identified which, together, will answer this. But you may still be unclear about precisely how to link these RSQs with the chapter structure of the thesis. This is the purpose of this chapter.

The first point, already noted but well worth repeating, is that RSQs can contribute greatly to the direction of chapters. For example, simply using the RSQ in the title of the chapter provides much greater focus and purpose to its structuring and writing. If you only provide titles for thesis chapters like 'Philosophy of science', 'Harlow's Research' or 'Castle Construction', you are in danger of leaving the reader (and yourself) without any clear sense of what the chapter will address. Better titles for these examples then might be the following:

The evolution of thought on a philosophy of science;

And

> Harlow's research on maternal deprivation: An ethical critique;

And

> Causes for the development of Castle Construction in France in the late Middle Ages.

Creating a chapter title with a relevant RSQ firmly embedded within it ensures that a chapter has both appropriate purpose and firm direction. And this doesn't just benefit particular chapters: by using an RSQ to determine chapter direction, you also ensure that the direction of the chapter feeds into the overall structure of the thesis, which is that of using the various RSQs to answer the MRQ.

Your chapters, then, if their titles, purposes and directions are clearly thought through, can provide strong bases from which to answer your MRQ. To develop this theme, this chapter of the book will therefore address the following issues:

1 What do standard empirical and non-empirical thesis structures look like?
2 Six groups of thesis chapters.
3 Linking the RSQs with the chapter structure of the thesis.
4 Examples of linkages from successful theses.
5 Applying this approach to the RSQs for your own thesis.
6 Spending your thesis words appropriately.

What does a standard empirical thesis structure look like?

Let's begin then by getting some sense of what a standard empirical thesis tends to look like. We'll begin by looking at the chapter structuring of a thesis concerned with the way in which research scientists might view the nature of their field. It is based upon Kuhn's (1996) claim that scientists tend to research, as 'normal' scientists, in a fairly uncritical way within particular disciplinary paradigms, and explores how current their thinking is on the nature and purpose of scientific investigation. The thesis MRQ then is phrased as:

> What philosophies of science do research scientists most embrace?

The research rationale of the empirical thesis is then to provide an analysis of the evolution of thought in the philosophy of science, use different historical versions to create particular statements about the nature and purpose of scientific enquiry, and then ask research scientists to record which statements they most agree and disagree with, in order to see with which schools of thought they most closely align.

The rationale of the non-empirical thesis on this issue might be to provide a similar analysis of the evolution of thought, but then to move to use new writers and new insights from papers and doctorates to suggest a new way of developing Kuhn's ideas of normal practice and paradigms.

Sorting out the thesis order

So below, the order of the chapters in an empirical thesis has been mixed up, as well as other sections like the appendices and references. The question to you is simply this: Can you arrange them into a more logical order? You might find it useful to do this in discussion with a colleague as an exercise in a notebook, on a computer or each of these chapters can be written on strips of paper and then arranged manually.

The jumbled chapters and sections of this empirical thesis then are:

- Appendices
- Five models of a philosophy of science
- References
- Conclusions and Recommendations
- Critiques of 'normal' scientific practice

- Contents

- Introduction

- Methodological issues

- Results

- The evolution of thought on a philosophy of science

- Analysis and Discussion

When you've examined these and decided on their order, put 1 next to the first section you think should be in the thesis, 2 next to the second, 3 next to the third and so on.

Here is a suggestion for the thesis structure:

Contents
Chapter 1: Introduction
Chapter 2: The evolution of thought on a philosophy of science
Chapter 3: Five models of a philosophy of science
Chapter 4: Critiques of 'normal' scientific practice
Chapter 5: Methodological issues
Chapter 6: Results
Chapter 7: Analysis and Discussion
Chapter 8: Conclusions and Recommendations
References
Appendices

Compare what you wrote with our suggestion. Here are some reasons for the order given to such a thesis:

- A contents page, followed by an introductory chapter, usually begin a thesis.

- Important concepts are normally discussed before most other discussions, to ensure clarity about the meaning of terms being used in the thesis before any discussion of previous research, as some of this may use different meanings, which may be missed if the conceptual work isn't performed first.

- You will want to make sure that what you intend investigating has not already been researched. So you will want to check the literature(s) on these issues early on, and certainly before embarking on any empirical research.

- Before embarking on your research, you will want to justify the methods you adopted in collecting your data, and how you went about setting up the research. These – and other issues – are covered under 'methodological issues'.

- When you have investigated your topic, you will need to describe your results before you analyse and discuss them.

- Your conclusions will need to come before any recommendations you make from the research.

This doesn't mean to say that there are no other possible chapter orders, but if you want to diverge from this, you need to be able to justify why you want to do this.

For many non-empirical theses, as we saw in the last chapter with Wong's thesis, much of the same structure can be used, and many of the same chapters. The discussion of methodology, for instance, will be concerned with particular types of argument, and/ or by the use of particular thinkers' approaches, rather than the use of empirical research tools. The analysis and evaluation chapters, as with empirical theses, will be the principal means of pulling together earlier literatures, but in this case probably intensive conceptual methodological analysis, large-scale literature reviews, and final questions about the area in question. For this thesis, the critical analysis and evaluation RSQ will probably be something like:

> How does this analysis impact on notions of normal practice and scientific paradigms?

The order of chapters, then, may be something like:

Chapter 1: Introduction
Chapter 2: The evolution of thought on a philosophy
  of science
Chapter 3: Five models of a philosophy of science
Chapter 4: Kuhn's Critique of 'normal' scientific practice

Chapter 5: The nature of scientific paradigms
Chapter 7: Analysis and Discussion
Chapter 8: Conclusions and Recommendations
References
Appendices

Groups of thesis chapters

In the theses above, then, you should be able to see that there are different groups of chapters, and that these groups appear in virtually all theses:

i   The first chapter, the Introduction, is a 'loner', but still very important; it provides the overall focus and structure of the thesis, the reasons for the need for the thesis, the MRQ, the RSQs and the linkages to the thesis chapters.

ii The next group of chapters are commonly called 'literature reviews', or 'background discussion', or 'relevant contexts'; they also provide discussions of any conceptual arguments in key terms used; on any similar research already performed in the area; and on important contexts which might impact on the empirical research.

iii The third group of chapters are those concerned with methodology. For non-empirical theses, this chapter or group of chapters will likely describe the conceptual tools to be used. For empirical theses, there may be one, two or even three of these: they usually cover the justification of the research methods chosen; ontological, epistemological and ethical issues; and a description of how you went about your research, the problems you encountered and how you attempted to resolve them.

iv The fourth group are the results chapters: you need to begin by describing your results, follow this with their analysis and then discuss these results. As you do so, you will almost certainly need to refer back to some of the literature reviewed earlier to show how your research results agree with or differ from these earlier findings.

v   The conclusions and recommendation chapter is critical to the thesis, as this is this chapter within which you attempt to answer your MRQ through summaries and discussion of the answers to the RSQs. After answering your MRQ, you then need to discuss the recommendations you think arise from your results, the limitations of your research and what future research directions your findings suggest.

Whether you think of your thesis in terms of individual chapters, or in terms of the 'groups' of chapters above, you need to get to the stage where

a   you can see a thesis title, or an MRQ, and can fairly quickly work out what RSQs will be needed to answer it;

b   what chapters in the thesis you will need; and then,

c   what will be the purposes of your chapters if together they will answer the RSQs and MRQ; and finally,

d   be able to work out in what order these chapters will come in the thesis.

Linking the RSQs to the thesis structure

By now, you should feel reasonably comfortable working out what kinds of chapters you need in order to cover the RSQs of your thesis, and the order you would expect them to be in. Table 6.1 may be helpful in making this clearer.

On the left hand side of Table 6.1 are the RSQs you have arrived at. As mentioned earlier, their number can vary from thesis to thesis, from MRQ to MRQ, and indeed the number may change as the thesis develops. But it shouldn't take any time at all to write these out.

On the right hand side of Table 6.1, and currently not aligned with the left hand side, is a fairly typical chapter structure of an empirical doctoral thesis. We're assuming here that it's a fairly large thesis (perhaps over 75,000 words), and so it's likely to have three or more chapters on conceptual issues, literature review and relevant contexts. We've also assumed two methodology chapters and two result chapters. Of course, some theses have only two

TABLE 6.1 RSQs and Thesis Chapters

RSQs	Chapters
LR RSQ1	Introduction
LR RSQ2	Chapter 1: Literature review 1
LRQ RSQ3	Chapter 2: Literature review 2
Methodology RSQ	Chapter 3: Literature review 3
Results RSQ	Chapter 4: Methodology
	Chapter 5: Methodology
	Chapter 6: Results I
	Chapter 7: Results II
	Chapter 8: Analysis and Discussion
	Chapter 9: Conclusions, Recommendations, Limitations, Future Research

literature chapters, and only one methodology chapter, and one results chapter – and in the end, you should decide on the number of chapters, based on (i) the amount of material which needs covering, (ii) the variety of this material, (iii) the norm for chapters of theses in your discipline and (iv) the views of your supervisors.

As a general rule, we tend to think that 8,000–10,000 words are probably the maximum length of a chapter that the average person can read before their concentration starts to flag. This being the case, splitting long results chapters into two (or even three) chapters is probably a very good idea, and particularly if you have different sets of results – for example, from questionnaires and interviews. But once again, the content of the right hand 'chapter' side of Table 6.1 is a matter of choice, discussion, – *and justification,* as it is possible that your examiners may ask you to justify the structure, the chapters and the order of the chapters you have chosen. Even if they don't, you should still have justified these to yourself and your supervisors. In so doing, if you later undergo a viva, you will be much more confident in defending your thesis, and your examiners will note such confidence, and should increasingly come to believe that such confidence is justified. Even if you don't have a viva, knowing why you are doing what you are doing, and justifying this to yourself before committing it into your thesis, is essential to the production of a watertight thesis.

In Table 6.2, we have blended the RSQs and the chapters together, by adding particular RSQs to particular chapters.

By placing an RSQ in a particular chapter (e.g. RSQ1 in Chapter 1) we are saying: 'This RSQ will be answered principally by material in this chapter'. But also notice that an RSQ may be included in more than one chapter, as it may be part-answered in one chapter, and part-answered in another. RSQ1 is then part-answered in Chapter 1, but is also discussed in Chapters 8 and 9. Now locating RSQs within various chapters does two things:

i It makes you as a writer and researcher work out within which chapters the evidence for your RSQs will be located; as just noted, part of the answer might be answered through one of the literature reviews, part through some of your results.

TABLE 6.2 Linking Chapters to RSQs

Chapters and RSQs
Introduction
Chapter 1: Literature review 1. RSQ1
Chapter 2: Literature review 2. RSQ2
Chapter 3: Literature review 3. RSQ3
Chapter 4: Methodology RSQ4
Chapter 5: Methodology RSQ4
Chapter 6: Results I RSQ RSQ 5
Chapter 7: Results II RSQ5
Chapter 8: Analysis and Discussion; RSQs 1, 2, 3, 5
Chapter 9: Conclusions; RSQs 1, 2, 3, 5 Recommendations, Limitations, Future research

ii It means that when you arrive at your conclusions, and you answer your MRQ through your various RSQs, you will probably draw on more than your empirical results, as some of the literature you uncovered earlier may throw significant light on answering the MRQ.

Applying these ideas to your own thesis

So now, reproduce Table 6.3, either on computer or notebook, and then add in your own RSQs and chapters.

TABLE 6.3 My RSQs and Thesis Chapters

RSQs	Chapters
Literature Review RSQs	Introduction
a	Chapter 1: Literature review 1
b	Chapter 2: Literature review 2
c	Chapter 3: Literature review 3
Methodology RSQ: What is the best way of investigating these issues?	Chapter 4: Methodology
	Chapter 5: Methodology
Research RSQs	
a	Chapter 6: Results I
b	Chapter 7: Results II
	Analysis and Discussion
	Discussion
	Conclusions, Recommendations, Limitations, Future research

Write each of your RSQs in the appropriate places on the left hand side of Table 6.3; leave space so that, if you have more than three literature reviews, you have the space to list them. If you have got less than the three listed here, then delete those unused. We've given you a methodology RSQ which works for most theses, whether empirical or non-empirical, but alter this if you can derive a better alternative. Now write each of your Research RSQs in the appropriate places.

When you've done this, review your RSQs once again, and then, on the right hand side of Table 6.3, write down chapter titles reflecting the focus of your RSQs.

1 When you've filled in both RSQs and Chapters, look again at Chapter 1 and ask yourself: which RSQ or RSQs will be addressed in this chapter? Then in the box in which Chapter 1 is written, write in the RSQ or RSQs addressed within it. Don't write this in full: simply put in RSQ 1, RSQ 2 and so on.

2 Go through each chapter title box and ask the same question: which RSQ or RSQs will be addressed in this chapter? As you move beyond the literature and methodology chapters in Table 6.3, you should find you are increasingly including more than one RSQ in a chapter box.

3 When you've been through all the chapter boxes, you should have a set of RSQs and Chapters which harmonize and which fully address the MRQ.

By the time you've reached this stage, you should have a strong idea of what the thesis is about, and how and where you are going to answer the questions posed. If you were to do the Café exercise again (even just by yourself) we think you will find it a lot easier now than previously.

However, before we finish this chapter, we want to deal with two final issues.

A first stems from the fact that you may have stumbled across this book when you had already begun your thesis. Hopefully, you have liked what you have read, but you may not be sure how to combine our suggestions with what you have done already.

The second issue is one of word length: you've got your chapter order set out, you've linked these with the RSQs, but how much should you write in each chapter? This question is very important but relatively neglected: under-spending or overspending wordage can have large and unwelcome effects on the balance of the rest of the thesis.

Coming across MRQs and RSQs a little late into the thesis

It's not always the case that students read a book they need before they start their thesis, and they are therefore not always able to use it from the start of their thesis. It's quite possible, then, that you've first come across MRQs and RSQs at a later stage of your thesis. If so, then you may realize you could have some problems. We suggest five possible scenarios.

A   *I've started writing thesis chapters before working out the MRQ and the RSQs.*

If this is the case, if you've already written a couple of chapters, you need to set aside these chapters for a moment and go through the process of working out what your MRQ should be and what the consequent RSQs will be. And be certain that the MRQ you now work out really does ask what you want to research in the thesis.

When you've done this, you need to go back into your chapters and reflect upon whether they correspond with your newly engineered RSQs. If they don't, you need to decide whether the RSQs or the current chapters correspond more closely with your MRQ. It is highly likely that the RSQs will correspond more closely with the MRQ, and if this is the case, then you will need to change (and possibly rewrite) sections of the chapters to provide them with a purpose and focus that ties them more closely to the RSQs. If you engage in rewriting by making your chapter titles the RSQ questions, and you refer to them constantly, you'll be able to see more clearly the extent of the changes required.

B   *I've been writing about what really interests me, and not what I have formally agreed to.*

If (a little surprisingly) these chapters better reflect what you would really like to research, then you need to stop and have some fairly prompt discussions with your supervisors. If you are engaged on a funded doctorate, where its purpose should be largely decided by a larger research project, or by the purposes specified by your funder, you may want to change the MRQ, and therefore the RSQs, but this clearly has wider implications than just your personal preferences. To repeat: urgent discussion is needed here. If, however, yours is not a funded doctorate and therefore you have more flexibility than this, then it may be easier to change MRQ and RSQs, but this is likely to make quite a difference to the focus of the thesis, the chapters and the planning for any empirical research. Once more, this requires prompt discussion with your supervisors.

C   *I picked up this book when I was half way through my thesis, and I've not constructed any RSQs.*

If this is the case, as before, you can construct your RSQs by deconstructing your MRQ. If you haven't formally constructed an MRQ, you should nevertheless have a fairly strong idea of it by now, and should do this formally as soon as possible. If you do have an MRQ (and may have called it the *central research question*, or the *main research focus*, or some such), then you can construct your RSQs by examining how this MRQ relates to the focus of the chapters you have already written. You may need to adjust all three (MRQ, RSQs and chapters) until you reach satisfactory agreement between them.

D   *To be honest, I've only got a general idea of the focus of my thesis, have only a few or no RSQs and only some chapter drafts.*

Well, it's clear you need to speak to your supervisors urgently, and you're going to have to engage in a fair amount of comparison and iteration between MRQ, RSQs and chapters, in order to ensure that all three of them harmonize. As already suggested, you need to return to the start of the thesis, work out a fairly tight MRQ, and the resultant RSQs, and then see whether these can harmonize with existing chapters, or whether they, the RSQs, or perhaps the MRQ, need adjusting.

E *I'm using an 'Aims and Objectives' approach, but really feel that an 'MRQ and RSQs' approach is a better way to go.*

There seem to be a couple of issues here. A first is that you may be using an approach entitled 'aims and objectives', but you are actually doing what is performed in this book. In other words, the thesis has a central aim, and the objectives are deconstructed from the aim, such that together they answer this central aim. If this is the case, then there should be no problem, and we suggest you carry on. But if you feel there is insufficient synergy and symbiosis between your aims and objectives, then you need to engage with your supervisory team and suggest a revisiting of the aims and objectives of the thesis such that the synergy and symbiosis between them becomes much stronger and clearer.

'Spending your words' in theses of different lengths

Now you may feel that once you've got your thesis chapters, your MRQ and your RSQs sorted, then you've got most of your initial structural concerns sorted. Yet we think there is one more important issue, too often neglected, which is well worth spending time thinking about. It is the issue of how many words should be spent in different parts of a thesis.

Now many students may not realize that this is a good question to ask from the very start of a thesis, because if considered and understood early on, it provides an indication of the number of words that should be 'spent' in particular areas of the thesis, and thus offers the student another valuable structural way of viewing each section of the thesis. Importantly, it also prevents the student from 'overspending' words in one section, and thus avoids the pitfall of having 'insufficient spending power' in others.

Now this book has argued that whilst there are some real commonalities between all doctorates, there are also some major differences between them, and the spending of words in particular sections is one such difference. They differ because doctorates differ in at least three ways. First, doctorates with different names can vary in the wordage required within the same country: wordage requirement in a PhD in England is different from wordage requirement for an Ed.D. A second difference is that a doctorate with the same name (e.g. PhDs) can have different word requirements in different countries. A final difference is that the same kind of doctorate in a country, or universities within that country, can differ in the wordage required in different disciplines (e.g. thesis lengths for different professional doctorates).

Because of these differences, it would be unhelpful and misleading to suggest appropriate chapter word lengths for different kinds of doctorates, just as it would also be inappropriate to suggest *percentage of thesis words* for the different areas in a doctoral structure.

Nevertheless, the principle of thinking this issue through for the doctorate you are tackling, within your particular discipline, and within the rubric of the university where you are doing your research, remains highly important. Discussion of appropriate chapter lengths then is relevant to virtually all doctorates, as inattention could result in an inappropriate balance between the chapters chosen to structure and answer the MRQ and RSQs.

This issue then should be given serious thought, and so requires at least two further actions. One is to review the length of similar doctoral theses in your own disciplinary area, with an appreciation of the kinds of chapter wordage balance that they use. This doesn't make them perfect, but if they have been successful, then their examiners have in effect approved the wordage balances used. The second is discussion with your supervisors on the balance of words between chapters they think is usual within your discipline, and what they think would be appropriate for your thesis. Neither of these actions provides the final answer: it is your doctorate after all, and you should take responsibility for its content, structure and balance of words. As you may know, the worst answer you can give to an examiner's question at a viva is to say 'because my supervisor told me to do that'.

So if, as argued in this book, the *Introductory chapter* to the thesis is seen primarily as an explanation of the genesis of the MRQ, the resultant RSQs and the consequent chapter contents, then, though this focus is very important to an overall understanding of the thesis, the chapter can be relatively short. Whilst some doctorates may differ because of disciplinary demands, good reason needs to be given for adding more to such a chapter.

In terms of *Literature review chapters* (which include information on contexts, and concept definitions or clarification), the situation is rather more variable. In areas where a critical overview and analysis of literatures pertaining to the MRQ is required, you may need a number of such chapters. Where, however, less context, or less definitional discussion is required, there may be substantially less to write. The question for students then will be: what is 'normal' for doctorates in my discipline, and what advice do my supervisors have for me here?

Methodology chapters: As already noted, we tend to see methodology chapters as (i) justifying particular research methods or critical approaches, (ii) justifying particular ontological and epistemological positions taken and the writer's 'positionality'; and (iii) explaining and justifying how the actual research was conducted. However, different disciplines give different emphases to the consideration of these areas – particularly when it comes to more philosophical or 'positional' questions. So there are likely to be considerable variations between disciplines in terms of word length for these chapters. When little-known or critically contested approaches are used, this may expand the wordage; whilst wordage may be considerably reduced if the methodology has already been largely decided and justified by a wider research project within which the doctorate is situated. Once again, the advice has to be: consult other successful doctorates in your area, and consult your supervisors.

Results, analysis and discussion chapters: There are different kinds of results chapters, and different kinds of analysis and discussion chapters. Some are largely based on words to describe results, some very largely on figures. Some may have only one set of results to report; others may have results from different areas or different groups. Some may use only one investigative tool (e.g. questionnaires, or a hermeneutical approach), whilst others may use a triangulation of methods. Some may try to analyse and discuss only one set of results before moving to another, whilst others may try to report, analyse and compare all groups simultaneously. Large variation is therefore to be expected.

How you decide to structure your results chapters to report these results is largely a matter of choice, but it must be a justified choice.

And whichever approach you take, there is likely to be considerable variation in the wordage needed to report the results and analysis chapters. Once more, the advice must be: consult similar theses in your discipline, and consult your supervisors.

(v) *The Concluding Chapter*: As with the introductory chapter, if you follow the argument of this book, and report the results of your RSQs, and use these to answer your MRQ, then this can be a highly focused section of the thesis. But individual theses require individual responses, and research on similar doctorates, and conversations with your supervisors will still be very important. In the same chapter come relatively brief sections on *recommendations, limitations and future research*. However, once again, their length depends upon the subject investigated, the implications from the results and the discipline within which the research is undertaken, and so the recommendation to research this further remains.

In summary, then, if you spend too many or too few words in one section of a thesis, you may unbalance the overall structure and create problems for yourself later down the line. To achieve a workable structure, you need to ensure that you maintain a balance in wordage between the different elements of the thesis. If you produce pieces that are much shorter than normal for your discipline, your reader may think that you haven't covered enough in the area or haven't engaged sufficiently in critical discussion. On the other hand, producing pieces that are much longer than normal may well suggest that you are not being selective or focused enough in what you write. If you find yourself writing wordages which differ significantly from the norm in your area, you need to discuss this with your supervisors, and see if they think there is a problem here, and if so, what needs doing about it. However, having said this, two points need repeating, whatever decisions you take:

a Ensure that you provide detailed justifications for them;

b Remember that these are your decisions, not your supervisors', and you are ultimately responsible for them.

So, finally ...

You are now in a position where you've managed to construct not only a thesis title, but an MRQ, and RSQs as well, and can therefore explain with some ease what your thesis is about. You have also made sure that your chapter titles correspond with the focus of your MRQ and RSQs. You've also now got a strong idea of the chapter structure of your thesis, just as you've got a good idea of approximately how many words should be 'spent' in each section.

And now you have one final act of structuring to do, and this involves going back through the chapter groups mentioned earlier, and reflecting on how their content and structuring can add to the overall thesis structuring. So the next chapter will examine how the introductory chapter can be most usefully structured, before we move systematically through the other chapter groups. You'll then be in a position to write a really strongly structured thesis – which any reader or examiner will thank you for.

CHAPTER SEVEN

Structuring the early chapters

Introducing the structure to others

Chapter 6 showed how you, the writer, can help others to understand the logic of your thesis structure. It described how and in which chapters, each of your Research Sub-Questions (RSQs) would be addressed. In the process, it made it clear that the chapters of your thesis are not independent and self-standing. Instead, you need to see them, and write about them, as parts of an integrated whole, each one of which contributes to the final full answer to your Major Research Question (MRQ). Here, then, we look in some detail at how the early chapters can make this contribution.

You'll remember that we suggested in the last chapter that there were different kinds of thesis chapters:

i the introduction, a 'loner' which lays out some personal issues, the main research questions and the thesis structure used to answer these;

ii the chapters concerned with discussions of disciplinary literature, or research background, or relevant contexts;

iii the methodology chapters, which cover the research methods chosen; ontological and epistemological positions taken; and how the research was conducted;

iv the results chapters, which describe the results, their
    analysis and their discussion, with reference back to earlier
    literature;

v   the conclusions and recommendations chapter: a critical
    chapter for the thesis, as the MRQ is finally and fully
    answered here. Besides conclusions, it normally also has
    sections on recommendations, research limitations, and
    future research directions.

In this chapter, we'll go through the first two kinds of chapters. But
these shouldn't be the first things you write for your thesis. It is *not*
a good idea to get all your materials together (literature, research
instruments, results, analysis), and only *then* begin to write them
up. As noted earlier, Guccione and Wellington (2017, p. 89) argue
that there are a series of writing 'gears' that the student needs to go
through, and you cannot begin to practice these too early. 'Lower
gear' writing processes involve skills like describing, paraphrasing
and summarizing things you've read; 'middle gear' processes involve
higher-level skills like interpreting, contrasting and connecting
different materials; whilst 'top-gear' writing processes involve skills
like synthesizing, categorizing, critiquing and developing your own
point of view. You then need to practice the skills of writing from
the very beginning. You get better at it by doing it; leaving it to the
end not only obstructs the thesis' iterative nature, it also prevents
the development of the critical skills of writing.

However, when it comes to writing drafts of actual chapters,
because the critical role of the introductory chapter is to provide the
reader (and the writer) with a clear understanding and structure to
the thesis, this, almost inevitably, has to be the first fully structured
chapter. It is to this then that we now turn.

The introductory chapter: Getting your suitcases on a train

After the last paragraph, it may seem a little strange to now say
that there is some truth in the well-worn saying that just about
the last thing you write in a thesis is its introduction. For those
who haven't heard this before, it may sound slightly crazy, but it

refers to the iterative nature of thesis construction: you may have a carefully planned thesis, but all kinds of things happen between writing the first and last pages. The former British Prime Minister Harold Macmillan was once asked by a young journalist whether there was anything likely to deflect him from delivering his policies. He smiled urbanely at the journalist and simply said 'Events, dear boy, events'. Theses are no different, and for a student who very probably hasn't researched and written one before, you need to expect the unexpected. So it's unwise to write an introduction, and then think that you've now completed this part of the thesis. Better to write the first draft of an introductory chapter, communicate to the reader a strong understanding of the thesis' central focus and structure, but accept that there will almost certainly be changes to this as the thesis develops. In truth, then, probably one of the last things you will write in a thesis is the *last* draft of its introduction.

But what are you initially going to put in it? You've probably got lots of ideas for the thesis, but how are you going to order them, so that they make strong coherent sense to your reader? After all, you don't want your examiners to start reading your thesis and come away after reading this chapter thinking that the thesis organization and structure are incomprehensible. First impressions are very important.

And this is a challenge that many thesis writers have faced. One of this book's authors when he was writing *his* PhD (Bottery, 1986) was told by his supervisor that his introduction was like someone embarking on a long train journey. It was suggested to him that all the necessary things for the journey were probably there, like suitcases on a railway platform, but reading the thesis introduction was like watching someone who hadn't worked out how to get these suitcases onto the train. As is usual with doctoral supervisors' comments, students, on initially hearing them, don't always fully understand what is said. Of course, my supervisor was trying to say, in the nicest way possible, that I had all the material to make a strong thesis, but I simply hadn't worked out how to introduce it to my readers. In effect, he was suggesting, he was watching me pick up some suitcases, and put down others, put some in the carriage, take them out again and put others in instead, because I hadn't fully thought through the purposes of what I was trying to do, and what would be the best means of achieving this. Not the way, you might think, to impress a spectator, or indeed the reader of the thesis.

So, the key question for a thesis introductory chapter is simply: what is its purpose? Well, it has more than one. We want to suggest that it has at least three.

The first purpose is for the writer to introduce themselves to their readers. We're not talking about a chapter of autobiography, but we do believe that one facet of doctoral training, and one criterion for the assessment of a doctorate, is the degree to which an individual changes and grows through engaging with the doctoral process. And many times, part of such development can be provided by the writer telling the reader why they became interested in this area of research, why it is an important area to develop further and why they are a suitable person to do this. If you're going to do this, then an introductory chapter is a very good place to do it.

Now just as we don't recommend autobiographies in introductory chapters, we are also not supervisors or examiners who like the over-liberal use of the word 'I' in a thesis, as it can conflate the personal with the material being researched. It has to be said that some disciplinary areas are more comfortable with the use of the word 'I' than others, and as with a number of other issues raised in this book, it is worth the student sounding out their supervisors on this. But certainly, at the start of the introduction, using the first person to let the reader know that there is an individual carrying out this research, and why they are the right person to do this research, can help tell a story not only of the development of this research, but of the researcher as well. So, going back to the train analogy, the first suitcase, so to speak, is a personal one, whose label states:

- Who I am, what I'm interested in researching and why I'm the right person to do this research.

But there's another part of you that you also need to get on board, and this is so important in many studies that it is worth providing it with a suitcase all of its own. It is what is technically called your 'positionality': in other words, the personal 'baggage' you bring to the doctoral journey through your background, your values, your hopes, your expectations and the reflection and discussion of how these might affect what you see, hear, write and interpret, and also the nature and content of the investigative tools you adopt. Very few doctorates are unaffected by this, and it is a good exercise and strong indicator of your reflexivity, to spend a little time discussing these issues. So the label on your second suitcase states:

- Who I am, and how this may affect my understanding of the area, and the research I am going to conduct.

If you start like this, you can now move almost seamlessly from a personal introduction into leading the reader into the subject matter of the thesis, moving from stating the general area of research in which you are interested, to the principal concern of the thesis. And from there it is a thoroughly logical move to state what the Major Research Question of your thesis is going to be. Your third suitcase then concerns your MRQ, and its label will say the following:

- My Major Research Question is then_____.

You've done this already. We introduced you to people like Sharron and her tame and wicked investigation of prison education; to Mike and his investigation of the potential of educational computer games, and to Jeff with his investigation of the theoretical background to building a greater social understanding of sustainability. We doubt you will have found these stories boring: it's a very human thing to understand the world through personal stories, and each doctoral thesis is a personal story, which leads into a major research question. And whilst up to now you've only got your first three suitcases on the doctoral train, you've pulled the reader into your story, you've justified why they have been chosen and you've justified putting them there in the order you specify. Your introductory chapter then is well under way.

Now it's very likely that if you have really taken on board what we've said in previous chapters of this book, then you will know what your fourth suitcase is going to contain. As covered in earlier chapters, to answer your MRQ, you're going to have to deconstruct it in order to provide a number of research sub-questions, which you will need to list and justify. These RSQs – and their justification – are then the contents of your fourth suitcase, and its label is clearly the following:

- These are the Research Sub-Questions which are needed to answer my Major Research Question.

We hope you are convinced that the advantage of this kind of introduction is to clearly and logically provide you the writer, and therefore your reader, with an argued movement from person to the area of study, to the main focus of the research, and then on to the questions that need answering if this main focus is to be properly addressed.

So far we've only mentioned four suitcases, and from what has been discussed in previous chapters, a fifth suitcase still needs to go on board. You've got a suitcase on board describing your personal motivation, qualifications and area of interest; another which describes your personal values and where you are 'coming from'; a third is the suitcase detailing the formation of your MRQ, and now you've got your RSQs suitcase on board as well. But now you need to locate where in the thesis these RSQs will be addressed, and that is the job of the fifth suitcase, which will be labelled:

- These research sub-questions will be answered in the following chapters.

By doing this, you've managed to get all your thesis structuring on board from its start, in an order which explains clearly and logically to the reader what you're doing, why you're doing it and how you're going to do it. By so doing, to continue the train analogy, you've given your readers a pretty full description of the journey you're taking them on. And we probably can't say too strongly: *your examiners will like you very much for doing this*. You've laid out the journey for them to follow, and they can therefore judge very easily:

a whether this is a suitable journey and destination for a doctorate;
b whether it's a suitable journey for you;
c whether you stick to that journey;
d how well you accomplish it.

These are exactly the kinds of questions they need to ask in judging your doctorate, and by providing them with this kind of introduction, you've made the job that much easier for them. And as importantly, by being so structured, if they accept your description of the journey and the destination, they are going to find it very difficult to pick fault with it. The watertightness of your thesis is being established in your very first chapter. Moreover, because you've made the job so much easier than it might have been, they will likely be looking quite kindly on your work after reading such an introduction.

Iteration and reflexivity

Having said that, your examiners won't be impressed, if you set out with a plan, and then stick rigidly to it, if it's obvious that it should have been adjusted. Such change may be required for a variety of reasons, of which these are just a few:

- Further reflection on an MRQ (e.g. *Investigating the impact of a new business technique on a hospital's functioning*) suggests the need for a literature review not considered initially (perhaps a literature review on the management of change in businesses), which then affects the kinds of data required and the methods used to acquire this data.

- A review of the literature on possible methods to investigate firemen's views of recent legislation in their area suggests that one-to-one interviews will be less effective than the use of small focus groups.

- A new understanding of how your 'positionality' affects the nature of your thesis, and necessitates a number of changes or additions.

- A student investigating a topic gets a much smaller response rate to her questionnaires than she anticipated, and possible changes or additions to data collection may then be needed.

- Simple good luck allows a student to have access to a number of ministry officials and their views on a major political change of forty years ago, so widening the stakeholder groups she intended using.

Some of the examples above are likely to require major changes in the orientation of the thesis, and each needs discussing thoroughly with supervisors. Other changes may be less impactful, but still need considerable reflection, as even relatively minor changes can still have effects beyond the changes themselves.

And beyond major changes and adjustments, there are the equally necessary reflections and adjustments needed as you come across an extra report or piece of literature, have discussions with supervisors and colleagues, or simply re-read what you have written so far, and see it with new understanding. This may mean subtle adjustments to a research sub-question, as it then better answers the MRQ, or it may mean an adjustment to the MRQ. However, you then need to ask yourself whether a change to the MRQ from an adjustment to an RSQ require adjustments to other RSQs. Some of these changes will be included in appropriate chapters, and as you describe the changes you've made, you are adding to the picture you presented at the beginning of the developing thinking processes of a new researcher. Other changes will simply mean adjustments to chapter structures or arguments, but crucially, they mean that you should never assume that what you initially write in your introductory chapter – or indeed in the rest of the thesis – is set in stone. Iteration and reflexivity are hallmarks of a robust, defensible and watertight thesis; those that lack these qualities are likely to read and be written too rigidly, too dogmatically, and the thesis will suffer accordingly.

Writing the introduction to your thesis through five luggage labels

Now that you've got the structure of the introductory chapter, you can write the introductory chapter for your own thesis. You'll find you've done most of this work already.

Remember, you've got five 'luggage labels' for your introductory chapter, and you now know their order, and the logic for this order. The labels are:

- Who I am, what I'm interested in researching in this area, and why I'm the right person to do this research.

- Who I am, and how this may affect my understanding of the area, and the research I am going to conduct.

- My Major Research Question is then_____.

- These are the Research Sub-Questions which are needed to answer my Major Research Question.

- These Research Sub-Questions are answered in the following chapters.

Remarkably for such an important chapter, as noted earlier, it can and should be really quite short. Describe the logic of the five labels, say what you have to say about them, say what the next chapter will be about and then move on. Your reader doesn't need and probably doesn't want more than this.

Now you've already covered much of this work in earlier chapters of this book. For instance, you've already covered the third label – the formation of the MRQ – in Chapter 4. You covered the fourth label, on the formation of the RSQs in Chapter 5. And the fifth label, on linking the research sub-questions to the chapters of the thesis, is covered in Chapter 6.

We therefore strongly suggest that you write the first draft of your introductory chapter now. It may take you a little while, but it's a really good thing to do whilst all of this is fresh in your mind. It will almost certainly require some adjustments later, but you will have a structured and argued basis for your thesis to refer to as you develop your thinking.

Importantly, in a final paragraph to this introductory chapter, now describe what will be covered in the next chapter, and why this needs covering at this point in the thesis. With these final few words, you reinforce the message that all chapters have specific functions which feed into the major concern of the thesis – to adequately answer your major research question. In writing this chapter, then, you've begun your doctoral journey for real.

Writing the 'literature reviews'

You'll have seen that whilst we've tended to use the term 'literature review' to describe early chapters in a thesis, we've also used other terms, as we aren't entirely convinced by the appropriateness of this name for these early chapters. In an empirical thesis, they usually come after the introduction and before the methodology discussions. In a theoretical doctorate, they can be located wherever a new area is covered, and may indeed form the bulk of the thesis. But you'll have seen that at times we've used other terms – for example, 'background' and 'context' to describe these chapters. There seem to be a number of issues which need dealing with here.

A first issue is that describing a chapter as a 'literature review' can suggest that the writer is using the chapter to review a specific body of academic literature. So if someone was investigating the causes of cancer, one 'literature' might be a review of relevant knowledge in the area of study, but as there are many causes and many cancers, perhaps this needs to be preceded by a discussion of what is meant by cancer, and what cancers will be referred to in this thesis. Similarly, if someone was investigating the viability of democracy in a former soviet country for their doctorate, it seems very likely that before one looked at this issue empirically, one would need to be very clear about what was meant by the term 'democracy'. These examples suggest the need for *conceptual exercises in examining key words in the study*. And even if the meanings of the terms 'cancer' and 'democracy' were agreed, there would be need to examine *the contexts within which these phenomena were investigated*, if particular contexts not only affected the conduct of the study, but the effects of the chosen concern. And as noted earlier, even then, the problem of which contexts still remain: Geographical? Historical? Cultural? Gender? Institutional? Indeed, not only might a number of contexts need discussing, but the contexts selected need justifying.

Second, an RSQ might contain elements of the disciplinary, the conceptual and the contextual. For example, if an MRQ was

What is the contribution of mobile technology to effective policing in Birmingham, Alabama?

One RSQ might well be: *What is meant by the term 'mobile technology'?* If this was the case, one might need to consult three different kinds of 'literatures': the definitional/conceptual issue of what mobile technology is; the disciplinary literature on how mobile technology has impacted on 'effective' policing (and 'effective' will need definition as well); and the contextual literature, reviewing its use in the United States, and particularly in Alabama.

Exercise: Can you do the same thing for the RSQs of a successful Irish PhD (McQuillan, 2011): Can you write next to the RSQs whether they are conceptual, disciplinary or contextual? The agreed MRQ was as follows:

What were the views of the first cohort of lay principals on their role in selected Catholic schools in Ireland, with particular emphasis on issues of management and organisational transition?

The literature RSQs were the following:

RSQ1: *What is distinctive about Catholic Education?* (Conceptual, Contextual or Disciplinary?).

RSQ2: *What is the historical role of the lay teacher in the Irish Catholic Secondary School System?* (Conceptual, Contextual or Disciplinary?).

RSQ3: *Which theoretical frameworks concerned with management and organizational transition would best inform this study?* (Conceptual, or Contextual, or Disciplinary?).

For RSQ1, it seems likely that all three would need including; for RSQ2, we think the main area would be largely contextual, with some disciplinary discussion; whilst RSQ3 would seem to be a mixture of the conceptual (because of the notion of theoretical frameworks) and the disciplinary (because these frameworks are largely located and discussed within disciplinary literature). We suggest that you perform the same exercise on any MRQ and RSQs in this book.

But a third issue now arises – in which 'literature review' chapter order should they be addressed? We've already suggested that definitional issues tend to come first because they help clarify what is being researched. However, when it comes to disciplinary and contextual chapters, there are no hard and fast rules, and you may well write them in one order, but then decide that they read better when they are placed in a different order. Having said that, it is probably more usual to write a predominantly disciplinary chapter before a contextual chapter, if only because the disciplinary review lets the reader see early on the grasp the writer has of the problems in their field, and because the context chapter begins the process of modifying this overview to the specific focus of the thesis. But if you feel strongly about this – *and can justify using a different order* – then go ahead. Just remember the need for really solid justification.

Critical selection or extensive coverage?

And this leads us into our final issue, which is about what needs covering in these chapters. As a general rule, we've found that if a student doesn't really understand what they should be doing in any or all of these chapters, whether we're talking about conceptual concerns, disciplinary issues or contextual factors, they will probably be tempted to try and cover as much as possible in the area with which they are concerned.

The first consequence will be apparent within a page or two: the reader is provided with something a little like a furniture catalogue. Or, to change the metaphor, and as Rudestam and Newton (1992, p. 49) said, you should build an argument not a library. The reader really doesn't want a review which simply details what Smith said, what Khan said, what Wright said and so on where there is no progress through the kinds of writing gears described above; and if only low gears are engaged, the chapter will fail to address the central purposes of a literature chapter. When this happens, the literature is managing the student. This may seem a strange thing to say, because literatures aren't conscious beings, able to direct the activities of other conscious beings. But their very presence can be so commanding, particularly if they are written by professors with doctorates, and located in prestigious journals in imposing libraries. Students may then feel that their job is simply to reproduce what is in the literature. Who am I, they may think, a lowly doctoral candidate, selecting among this material, criticizing these eminent people? In addition, it is a lot harder to write a selective critique of a literature than it is to simply summarize what you have read.

And yet it is essential that you, the student, run the literature: to recognize that if you can justify your selection and your critique, then you have every right to decide what goes in, what comes out and what you say about it.

Once again, this is where RSQs are so very useful, because they provide the writer with a purpose and a direction to seize this almost hypnotic initiative and control away from the literature. Without RSQs, a thesis title/MRQ might be really difficult to unpick. Take, for instance, a thesis with an MRQ like

> What are the effects of a high-trust culture on individuals at different levels in selected sportswear businesses?

What kind of RSQs, and therefore chapters, will the doctoral candidate need in order to answer this major research question? Without the deconstruction of this MRQ, they may well write early chapters with titles like *Literature Review 1*, *Literature review 2*. Slightly better, but still relatively simple, they may use titles like:

- the nature of high-trust cultures;
- the nature of sportswear businesses.

These are reasonable chapter titles, but they don't necessarily provide a full array of answers to the MRQ, which may initially be deconstructed into a set of RSQs like the following:

RSQ1: What constitutes a high-trust culture?

RSQ2: In what ways does a business ethos impact on a high-trust culture?

RSQ3: In what ways is a sportswear business ethos distinctive?

RSQ4: How do hierarchies impact on trust relationships?

RSQ5: What are the effects on individuals at different levels of a business?

RSQ6: What are the best means of investigating these issues?

Devising such RSQs – and reflecting upon them and changing them if necessary – will deepen an understanding of what is needed in particular chapters, and crucially, will focus the reading, research and writing of the student on answering these RSQs. On no occasion in a doctorate, then, should the candidate be reviewing all of the material in the area under consideration. Instead they should be selecting only that information which enables them to answer the specific RSQ being addressed. The student's primary task then is one of structuring these chapters in such a way that they selectively critique a literature on the discipline, the concepts or the context, to answer a specific RSQ, and therefore to ultimately answer the MRQ. RSQs then are enormously helpful in facilitating the critical selection and focus required for writing thesis chapters.

We've now covered the early chapters, the ones that inform the reader of the intentions of the thesis, the structure which delivers these intentions and the influence of important literatures and contexts upon this piece of research. To now embark upon gaining your own data, you will need to inform your readers of the principles that inform your research, the methods and techniques that are most appropriate to gather this data and how you intend to gain it. You are moving into the vital linking chapters where you discuss your methodology.

CHAPTER EIGHT

Structuring the middle chapters

Introduction: The meanings of methodology

The middle chapters of your thesis comprise the connecting bridge between the earlier work on your research questions, the literature and context chapters and the data you collect to answer these research questions. This bridge then is a 'methodological bridge', normally located in these middle chapters in order to enable you to provide a convincing description and justification of how you are going to conduct your research in ways appropriate to the nature of your research questions. Now we say 'normally', because as noted earlier, with Wong's thesis (2005), it is possible for a conceptual methodology chapter to be located earlier in a thesis, for if the methods used are conceptual in nature, the explanation of their use needs to come early on.

This also has implications for the meaning of 'methodology'. We see it as an overarching term, embracing limited or extended discussions on four different issues:

1 the selection and justification of methods and techniques used in gathering your data, including philosophical ones;
2 the application of concepts like validity, reliability, generalizability, and trustworthiness to improve the confidence that others have in your findings;

3 the manner and degree to which personal, cultural, and ethical values may affect your research;

4 the description of the practical application of your chosen methods and techniques to the problem you are investigating.

Now we say 'limited or extended discussion' because there are differing views on the importance of some of these issues. In some disciplines, and in some theses, methodological issues may be viewed as reasonably unproblematic. For example, in a doctorate funded through a research grant, and as a contribution to a larger team project, much thinking on the methods to be used will probably have been taken within the larger project overview. One might be tempted to call this an 'off-the-shelf' methodology for a doctorate, as it may seem to come as a pre-packaged, fully researched instrument, where the doctoral student needs to only ensure that a step-by-step guide to its implementation is followed, and from there to the collection and analysis of the desired data.

Yet there are two major problems with such an approach. First, if much of the methodological work is done before a student begins their study, it is debatable just how 'doctoral' their education will be. If one of the major purposes of engaging in a doctorate is to enable the student to grow as a researcher, then such an approach may well stunt such growth. The doctoral student then needs to be given the space and opportunity to understand the issues arising from the methodological considerations described above. Second, an examiner will very likely ask a range of methodological questions, and a doctoral candidate needs to be able to discuss and justify the approach taken within their thesis, and especially at any summative viva occurring at the end of the process. For these two reasons – the need for a doctoral education in methodological concerns, and a necessary justification of approaches taken – methodological issues need taking seriously.

Selecting techniques and methods

Ideally, most researchers would like to find out as much as possible about their research concerns, and empirically this can be done in two ways. First, they can try to extract data from as many instances of a phenomenon as possible. If so, they likely will research very broadly (quantitatively) into the subject matter, and probably record the data in terms of numbers. However, they could also go deeply and try to explore as much as possible about particular instances; in which case, they will very likely research qualitatively into selected individual instances, and probably record the data in terms of words.

Now many researchers, being limited in time and resources, may not be able to cover all the instances available, nor may they ever really know if they have gone sufficiently deeply to fully understand any particular instance. What tends to happen is that in quantitative research, either a sample number is claimed sufficient to derive a set of findings which are generalizable to the population; or in qualitative research, a situation is reached where researchers claim either that they are getting the same responses as with other instances, or they are not getting anything new from the same instance, both of which can be called a 'saturation' of data, and so they may claim that they do not need to go more deeply. These two approaches are illustrated in Figure 8.1.

Most doctoral candidates will be aware that 'wide' and 'deep' kinds of research are normally dealt with by using different research approaches: quantitative approaches for 'wide', qualitative for 'deep'. A fairly typical illustration of these differences is provided in Figure 8.2, where not only are the kinds of methods available on a quantitative/qualitative research methods continuum described, but so also are the problems and issues likely to occur when one or the other approach is adopted. Moreover, as Figure 8.2 suggests, the virtues of one approach tend to be the problems of the other. This suggests that the choice of a *triangulated* approach (a strange term, given that you may adopt only two, or more than three, different methods or techniques) may be the best way of avoiding

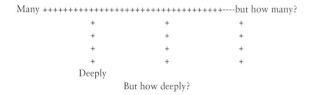

FIGURE 8.1 *A research methods continuum.*

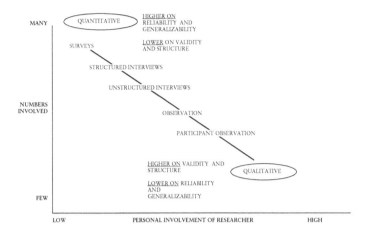

FIGURE 8.2 *Issues on a research methods continuum.*

such problems, and more inclusive and wide-ranging information may be produced. Triangulation – the selection and comparison of results from different methods – helps you to do this, and by using both kinds of approaches, you may go some way to offset the weaknesses of one approach with the strengths of the other. The awareness then of the purposes and scope of quantitative and qualitative approaches, and their strengths and weaknesses, needs to be part of any justification you provide for any single or triangulated choice of methods.

As a doctoral researcher, then, it's a good idea to stop here and ask yourself two simple questions:

- Which approach am I favouring?
- Why am I favouring this approach?

Provide an oral, and then a written answer to yourself, or better, to a knowledgeable friend. Be careful not to give either the answer 'because this is what everybody else in my area is doing' or 'because my supervisor told me to do it that way'. You need to be able to provide a justification which you can understand and defend, one which stems from the nature and the virtues of the particular approach, and not because it feels culturally comfortable, or because you feel you need to defer to the experience of your supervisors.

Choosing the right techniques to ensure the quality of your data

Now because quantitative and qualitative research methods are used primarily for different purposes, they shouldn't necessarily be judged by the same criteria. If, for example, you are trying to detect response patterns in a large population, this will require one approach; investigation of the underlying causations of such patterns may need a different and deeper approach. Similarly, if you are using an approach to understand the deeply held beliefs of a group of individuals, then the use of the same approach to detect larger patterns in such responses may be inappropriate. It is important then that you are aware of the range of concerns about research instruments – things like validity, reliability and trustworthiness – which may need detailed consideration when adopting particular methods or techniques. But you should also be aware of *which* issues from this range are important for your particular project in your own discipline, and which are not.

In summary, then, you may need different methods to get the best results for different issues (many or deep?) and if you want a really comprehensive overview of an issue, you may need both 'many and deep' approaches – and so need to triangulate your research instruments and findings. But you will need time to arrive at and justify such approaches – and new doctoral researchers may underestimate this requirement. The advice to doctoral researchers then is twofold. First, be aware of the time needed in which to complete your thesis, and fit the scale of your approach to the size, the time, the demands and the wordage of your doctorate. Second, be able to explain and justify why your research may need to be informed by only some of the issues listed above.

Issues of epistemology, ontology and positionality in different kinds of theses

Issues of epistemology, ontology and positionality can be daunting, as they are concerned with some of the most difficult doctoral questions, including the following:

- What is the status of the knowledge I am researching?
- What kind of a world view does such a view of knowledge imply?
- How much do I need to be concerned about my influence on the research?

Their perceived importance to thesis structuring can vary with the academic discipline, as outlined in Table 8.1 below. Thus, some researchers in the scientific disciplines may believe in a fairly objectivist view of knowledge, in the possibility of one world view (Chalmers, 2005), and the limited influence of the researcher on their object of study. They may therefore attach a limited importance to discussion of some of these concerns in the thesis. The social science disciplines, however, can be quite schizophrenic, with some researchers wanting to imitate the practice of the natural sciences and its attendant views on knowledge, world views and researcher influence. Others, however, will want to argue that the nature of their disciplines – that of investigating the reflective human being – requires the embrace of a fairly subjective view of knowledge, a belief in the likelihood of human beings holding different world views, and in the potential for their considerable researcher influence, conscious, or unconscious, on what they are studying.

TABLE 8.1 A spectrum of opinions on the nature of knowledge, reality and researcher involvement

	Greater belief that...	Greater belief that...
Knowledge	More objectivist view of knowledge is possible	More subjectivist view of knowledge is necessary
Reality	More 'realist' view of the world is possible	More interpretive view of the world is necessary
Researcher involvement	(i) Less personal framing is possible (ii) Less need for consideration of positionality	More personal framing is inevitable More need for consideration of positionality

The result is that these social science theses may give considerably more discussion to such issues in methodology chapters.

Now much of this difference stems from the perceived nature of the different kinds of subject matter that disciplines study, and therefore, the degree of 'objectivity' that researchers may feel they can claim for their findings. Most researchers in the scientific disciplines investigate aspects of the natural world which aren't aware of, or react to the intentions or actions of the researcher. These researchers would also probably argue that their disciplines have specific and very public rules concerning what constitutes 'scientific work', rules designed to eliminate individual bias from any research procedures. Such views, then, may be located towards the left hand side of Table 8.1. Now if it is believed that scientific data are much less contaminated by human influence than the data of social scientists, then such researchers may also believe that their data – and hence their 'epistemology' – is more 'objectivist' than the kind that social scientists explore. Their 'ontology' – their view of the world – may then be one claiming a much clearer apprehension of an external 'reality'. Indeed, through the nature of their subject matter, such physical scientists may have some justification for claims to greater 'objectivity' of their findings than social scientists, and perhaps therefore less inclination to want to have detailed discussion of such issues in a methodology chapter, believing that one less layer of interpretation is required.

Social Science disciplines, on the other hand, normally investigate issues in the human world, where as Bryman (1992, p. 79) suggests, many researchers are engaged in 'interpretations of other people's interpretations'. In addition, some social scientists argue that because human beings have brains which necessarily select from the stimuli in front of them, they generate different understandings or 'frames' of this world, and their knowledge – their 'epistemology' – is inevitably not 'objective' but a more 'subjectivist' product of what they select. This view of a social scientist's 'ontology' – how they view the world – is then very likely to accept that human beings never actually see a final version of 'reality', but at best interpret the stimuli they receive in order to construct their versions of it.

The history of many social science disciplines (e.g. psychology) is coloured by attempts to emulate the natural sciences, and to reject data that don't conform to natural science criteria (Shotter,

1975). Indeed, such a view worked its way into the world of philosophy (Ayer, 1940). Critics have accused them of losing much valuable data through restricting their focus in this way. Instead they argue that social scientists adhere to principles of logic, rationality, contestability and public discussion, just as natural scientists do, yet because they are heavily involved in investigating the framings of reality by other human beings, their research needs to include discussion of whether and how such framing can affect the research itself. They are thus much more likely to locate discussion of the content covered in the methodology chapter further to the right on Table 8.1. This can create some confusion, as researchers (and supervisors!) within the same discipline can take very different views on issues of ontology, epistemology and personal framing.

Such concerns, however, are not restricted to the thought and practice of the social sciences. It might be pointed out that at the heart of the physical sciences, Heisenberg's uncertainty principle established that the act of measuring atomic particles affects the direction they take and interferes with the accuracy of any measurement. And whilst the scientific method applies principles of logic, rationality, contestability and public discussion to move beyond personal opinion to arrive at publicly accepted scientific 'truths', researchers in the physical sciences are human beings like researchers in the social sciences, both of whom necessarily have to select from and frame any external reality. The fields of the history and philosophy of science, and particularly the work of individuals like Thomas Kuhn (1996) and Paul Feyerabend (1978) then, are replete with examples of how the practice of science can and has been heavily influenced by cultural and personal concerns. Perhaps they have more in common with writers on the philosophy of history, like E. H. Carr (1964), for instance, who argues that historians cannot stand outside the process by which they research the past, as they are necessarily affected by the views and values of the times in which they live. Kuhn, in his writing on the philosophy of science, similarly argues that cultural and personal values can influence scientific attitudes and approaches, resulting in many scientists (and doctoral students) unwittingly practicing what he calls 'normal science' within a particular scientific 'paradigm'. Scientific change then happens, but may result in little more than observance to a new paradigm.

This suggests a much less certain view of science, with people like Popper (1982, p.111) arguing that

> the empirical base of objective science has … nothing 'absolute' about it. Science does not rest upon solid bedrock. The bold structure of its theories rises, as it were, above a swamp. It is like a building erected on piles. The piles are driven down from above into the swamp, but not down to any natural or 'given' base; and if we stop driving the piles deeper, it is not because we have reached firm ground. We simply stop when we are satisfied that the piles are firm enough to carry the structure, at least for the time being.

Any novice doctoral researcher, then, may be influenced by 'normal' practice within their discipline, and by the position their supervisors take on such issues. It may be that a particular position within a discipline suggests little need for the inclusion of much discussion on such issues within a methodology chapter, yet doctoral candidates still need to be cognizant of such debates, and in deciding on and justifying the degree to which such issues *are* included in their methodological discussions. Issues of epistemology, ontology, and personal framing may be key elements of discussion within some methodology chapters, or they may be given little attention, but the justification of these decisions by the doctoral candidate seems essential either way.

Ethical Questions: Values also intrude through the conscious or unconscious positions taken on ethical issues like animal and human experimentation, on power and political positioning, on researching nuclear or biological weapons, and in the way in which the adoption of a particular research approach may lead to the neglect of other areas potentially more valuable to society. Awareness and discussion of these seem essential to doctoral discussion where relevant.

Ethical concerns can be focused on wider implications of a piece of research, but they can also be concerned with the manner in which the research is conducted. A doctoral candidate then needs to be mindful of and capable of informed discussion on whether the following kinds of issues are raised within their research, and how they are dealt with:

- the nature of the research project *(e.g. animal experimentation)*;
- the context of the research *(e.g. in a prison setting; in a school?)*;

- the nature of the procedures to be adopted *(e.g. pretending to be doing one thing while doing another?)*;

- the consequences of using procedures *(e.g. asking personal questions which may lead to personal distress?)*;

- the nature of the participants *(e.g. cognitively impaired adults? Those with different cultural views?)*;

- the type of data collected *(e.g. highly personal or sensitive data?)*;

- the use and abuse of data *(e.g. where it is published; whether some data are emphasized to achieve a desired result)*.

Most universities nowadays require compliance with ethical procedures and the submission of an ethics form in this respect, and the organization(s) in which your research is conducted may have their own ethical guidelines and procedures as well. In these forms you will be asked to explain what the research entails and how any ethical issues raised will be dealt with. There are a range of helpful texts and sources to which you can refer for more detail on this aspect (Israel, 2014; Barnaum and Byron, 2001; Resnick, 1998). With these issues in mind, it is now time to talk about the actual application of techniques and methods to a particular study.

Applying the techniques and writing about the unexpected

Having planned and structured all the things you think you need to do, and discussed these in detail with your supervisors, you probably want to get on with the research. But it is very important to commit to paper or computer such plans and structure, and a first full draft of these bridging issues should be completed before you actually begin. As you do so, you need to keep two issues in particular in mind.

A first one concerns how you intend presenting this bridging material in the thesis. Some researchers use separate chapters to write about the selection of methods, the philosophical and ethical issues and the actual conduct of the research. Others put them all together in one chapter. It is for the individual doctoral researcher to make final decisions on which is the more appropriate strategy, though an important consideration is the length of the material to be covered, and whether a reader would be helped by being given chapter breaks before reading different parts of this material.

The other issue concerns past and present tenses in your writing. Thus, when you write the first full draft of a methodology chapter, it is likely, because you won't yet have conducted the research, that it will be written in the future tense: 'I will send out these questionnaires to … , I will pilot my interviews by … .' However, when you have actually conducted the research and are writing the final drafts of your thesis, you need to address the reader in the past tense. As you do this, new material will be incorporated, in particular the unexpected things that you encountered:

> I intended sending out the questionnaires to … but I met a number of difficulties, and so …'; I intended piloting my interviews with … and managed to do this, but this resulted in some interesting changes to their wording.

The later drafts of this part of your thesis then should not only be in the past tense but also address the unexpected events that you encountered, and how you dealt with them, and in so doing these drafts should demonstrate that your thinking on these issues is more advanced than previously. The unexpected in research then throws up a number of issues, the specification and resolution of which may need inclusion in the thesis.

A first concern is how you decided which were the best sources for your data. The actual data, and the people from whom you want to gather data, are vital to your research, and whilst you will likely have covered in earlier drafts the reasons why you chose these examples, in later drafts you may need to cover whether there were any difficulties faced in doing this, and how you overcame them. One frequent problem here is that of accessing data or people. This often means talking about the 'gatekeepers', those individuals who provided you with this access, and you cannot write about any difficulties here until you have gone into the field and actually met these people. Some part of your writing then has to wait until you have engaged in your research.

Another issue concerns that of piloting materials. When you devise instruments to gather data, it is usually very important to test them out first in one or more pilot studies, and from the lessons learnt, make changes to your research instruments. You need to keep records from such piloting, such as the different drafts of questionnaires and interviews, changes arising from talking through an instrument with a colleague, or by actually practicing the technique on a willing volunteer. The details of the piloting, the lessons learnt and the changes made are then integral to discussions in your thesis about your developing understanding of research techniques' application.

There are also instances where what you actually did, differed significantly from what you had originally planned. Now it is perfectly normal for the unexpected to occur in the research process: indeed it would be a surprising thesis if this didn't happen on a number of occasions. If you have reflected upon these and discussed them with your supervisors, an event like this can be turned into a positive rather than negative contribution to the thesis, as it will demonstrate your ability to adapt to changing circumstances whilst still maintaining the integrity of your research purposes.

More problematic is when you realize that you might, on reflection, have planned something differently at the start of the thesis. Such a change of mind is really a reflection on the *justification of a choice*, and where your reflection on the thesis, as it nears its end, suggests you might have taken a different path. However, once again, this seems more like a development of your thinking on the research process, the experiential learning essential to any doctoral education, rather than an error per se. In such circumstances, then, the description – and justification – of your change of mind should be treated – and argued by you – as a positive rather than a negative indicator for the thesis. Whilst you want to create a watertight thesis, the occasional small leak, as with ships, is no disaster, particularly if it can be shown the structure is sufficiently sound to contain this leak.

Similarly, when something has happened over which you had no control, and which you now feel you might have dealt with better, it is highly unlikely that this will seriously damage your thesis, largely because of the structures you had already put in place.

Once again, if you now reflect with your supervisors on what you might have done differently, and on whether this ultimately affects the strength of your conclusions, you will display an approach of reflection, admission and learning which demonstrate the essentials of a student's doctoral growth. To use the watertight theme once again, you may have sprung a leak, but the strength of your overall structure will be sufficiently sound to make it very unlikely that the ship has major problems.

Final thoughts

The methodology section of a doctoral thesis, then, is the crucial connecting bridge between the earlier and later parts of the thesis, as earlier discussions of research questions are 'operationalized' through methodological considerations to produce the research data and thesis conclusions. The methodology section is then a vital part of the thesis, regardless of the discipline within which the thesis is written. By building a strong and convincing connecting bridge from the start of the thesis to the research data, once more you communicate to readers and examiners the structural strength of the thesis. It is time now to turn to the analysis and discussion of your data.

CHAPTER NINE

Structuring the later chapters

Introduction

The previous two chapters outlined the importance of developing a clear and watertight structure in the introduction, literature reviews and methodology chapters. This same emphasis on structure and clarity is possibly even more important in the later chapters, as they most strongly emphasize the teleological or goal-directed nature of the thesis. Having been structured to provide an answer to a key Major Research Question (MRQ), these are the chapters where this answer is provided. In them, you present the results of any empirical work, you develop a cogent discussion of your findings in the light of your answers to the literature Research Sub-Questions (RSQs) discussed earlier, and finally you detail your conclusions and offer recommendations.

In sum, this chapter suggests that the best way of structuring your later chapters is to do the following:

- Structure your results in such a way that you derive detailed answers from them to your relevant RSQs.

- Use the summaries of these full replies to the RSQs to synthesize an answer to your MRQ.

So, it is really worth emphasizing that a thesis using our approach is focused on answering a main research question, and this main research question is answered by its deconstruction into research sub-questions. So if you have gathered data which can provide answers to your RSQs, you can then answer your MRQ. This logic then should provide the essential focus and structure for these chapters. By doing so, you are not only providing an extremely clear guide to your examiners in how you are concluding your thesis but also significantly strengthening its watertightness.

This chapter then begins by dealing with the structuring of results, before it moves to their discussion, and then finally details how final conclusions and recommendations are arrived at.

A preliminary caution

Now, before we begin, it is important to point out that these later chapters can be the ones which students may be tempted to rush: they see the end in sight, they are normally very tired, and they just want to finish. However, rushing, or not reflecting sufficiently here, can seriously impair the quality of the conclusions drawn, and therefore damage the thesis. So, never, ever, be content with your first drafts. Once you have drafts of the answers to your RSQs and your MRQ, take a break, and then look critically again at the answers to each RSQ and to the MRQ, and any relationship between these answers, and if necessary redraft the problematic elements. It's then a good idea to leave them again for a day or so, come back with fresh eyes, and see how it all looks then, and if necessary, do a further redraft.

So now let's begin by looking at the structuring of your results.

Structuring your results chapter(s)

Once data are gathered, they need analysing. The details of procedures for empirical data are outside this book's scope, but there are plenty of texts (e.g. Miles and Huberman, 1994, Field, 2005) providing good guidance on this for the research student. The key issue – for both empirical and non-empirical theses – is how to structure the presentation of the results and to ask yourself: how do I make a coherent and structured chapter here? This can be a real headache with many students unsure of how to proceed. A first point is made through the true story of one diligent but unreflective student who turned up at our office reporting that he had analysed his data and proceeded to wheel in a shopping trolley containing the equivalent of about eight reams of paper printout! The first point, then, is that gathering results is not the same as analysing them. Whilst it is almost certainly impossible to incorporate everything from the results gathered, the more important element of analysis is not in simply reproducing in the thesis the data that has been gathered, but in *selecting* the appropriate materials from the mass of materials gathered.

But how do you make such a selection? This is a fundamental problem that many students struggle with. Without any real strategy, this critical part of the thesis, the part which provides the answers to your MRQ, might meander along, dwelling on some bits, moving to other issues, but without any coherent order or structure. We've talked before about your examiners' need for clarity in what you are arguing, and this would be a really crucial – and very sad – place to lose them now.

The resolution of such problems, as we've argued, lies in the fact that the selection of material and the structuring of the results are driven by your research sub-questions. You have already used some of these to interrogate your literature and context chapters and others to select your research instruments, and now you should use RSQs to select the really important data from those which are less so and which help you structure your results chapter(s) to answer these questions. These issues need expanding upon.

Let's begin with how answers to RSQs can help structure the answers to your questions. A good example comes from a successful doctoral Kuwaiti candidate (Alhatlani, 2018) who wanted to research the situation of stateless people. He devised a research sub-question which asked the following:

What are the perceptions of a sample of key personnel on the issue of education for the Bidoun in Kuwait?

The 'Bidoun' is a Kuwaiti term for stateless people, and he developed this concern into a detailed interview schedule of questions, enabling him to gather data with much fine-grained detail by conducting interviews with key people in Kuwait who held differing views on the subject. His first interview question invited his respondents to indicate how they understood the term 'Bidoun'. He then asked them how their understanding about this situation had developed. In writing up his data, he deliberately used his interview question schedule, which had been derived from his RSQ, to order and structure this section of his thesis. In this example, then, the RSQ suggested the nature of the interview schedule and the interview data gathered were structured following the interview schedule, and then used to answer his RSQ. In his viva, he was complimented by his examiners on how well he had dealt with the complexity emerging from the data.

A second example, which describes the structuring of the full process, comes from another successful candidate, Saeed Albuhairi (2015). Saeed had two MRQs:

> What is the prevalence of necessary preliminary factors in the development of cooperative learning in Saudi Arabia,

and

> What are the challenges and facilitatory factors in this development?

The following RSQs were derived from these MRQs:

- What is cooperative learning?
- What does research literature say about the necessary preliminary factors in the development of cooperative learning?
- What is the prevalence of the necessary preliminary factors in the Saudi context?
- What are the challenges to their development?
- What facilitating factors exist to aid their development?
- What are the best ways of investigating these issues?

The particular RSQs driving the empirical research were the following:

- What is the prevalence of the necessary preliminary factors in the Saudi context?

- What are the challenges to their development?
- What facilitating factors exist to aid their development?

Like Alhatlani (2018), Albuhairi used his interview schedules to structure the answers provided by his interviewees. By recognizing that he had three different groups to ask, and the need to provide data to three RSQs, he was able to structure a results chapter, which reported on the responses to each of these issues by his different groups. These results were then used to answer the RSQs that had driven the need for the data, and from the answers to the RSQs, he was then able to answer his MRQ. Empirical theses then have much data to gather and use in response to the RSQs. Non-empirical theses won't have data in the same way, but they will have important conceptual distinctions, arguments, new information and developments in thinking to report on in these later chapters. So in both kinds of theses, there may be much material which needs reporting and discussing.

When you come to the end of your results chapter(s), you should reflect on these results and provide a short summary in which you remind the reader of what you think are the important patterns which appear to be coming out of your data. Both you and your reader will be helped in this if, throughout your results chapters, you point out some significant details which suggest the emergence of such key trends. It can be useful to think of data in empirical theses – or arguments in non-empirical theses – as 'low-hanging fruit', because they are easily seen, easily extracted and easily remembered; they are therefore the right kind of data to reflect upon with respect to emerging patterns before the next chapter begins. Not unimportantly, some small commentary on these data during the chapter also maintains interest for the reader, for if all they read is an apparently endless stream of data, even well-structured data, this can become tedious and difficult to follow, and you don't want to create a bored examiner.

One final but important question then is: how many chapters should I use to present these results? There is no set rule here: some theses may take only one chapter, whilst others may take two or even three. However, an important consideration is that of needing to help your readers to understand your results. If, for instance, your study contains data from a large survey and a number of follow-up interviews, you may decide that this would be better presented as two chapters, one for each kind of data. On the other hand if you have a large body of interview data from three different sample groups, it might be sensible to present these as three separate chapters rather than as a very large – and possibly indigestible – chapter to your examiners. In a non-empirical thesis, the same concerns apply: decisions need to be made over whether different kinds of evidence and argument can be accommodated within the one chapter or need dealing with in more than one. This eventually is a matter of an individual judgement applied to a unique thesis.

Now, you may have noted that no mention has been made in the writing of this chapter to links with your earlier literature reviews. This is quite deliberate. Your results chapter should be restricted to the analysis and presentation of data, with some small preliminary discussion about them. How this relates to your earlier chapters on literature and context is best left until the discussion chapter, and this comes next.

The discussion chapter

For some students this can be the hardest chapter to write. The difficulties often stem from recognizing that this shouldn't just repeat what was dealt with in the results chapter, and yet students may still be unsure of how to frame it differently. Now there will always be some degree of repetition and re-presentation of data in a discussion chapter, if only to remind the reader of what will be discussed, but the chapter's central purpose is to present a new synthesis of the data which helps the reader understand how a data set or a preceding conceptual analysis helps answer the key questions of the thesis – first, the RSQs, and then the MRQ.

Part of the creation of this new synthesis comes from the analysis and discussion of the data itself and part comes from considering this new data in the light of earlier literature RSQs. Your new data or arguments allow you to build further on this literature and further enable you to develop new ways of considering the issue at the heart of your research. In so doing, you are moving from being a learner student in the discipline to becoming a genuine contributor and authority among your academic peers.

The answers that begin to appear in response to your research sub-questions thus provide you with a clear and logical basis for the structure of this vital chapter. But organizing this chapter can, once more, be a little like getting your bags on the train mentioned earlier: it's never easy to decide what goes on first. A good way of approaching this task is simply to talk it through before you commit anything to paper, as many people find that talking rather than writing frees up their mind and makes explanation much easier. So it's a good idea to get that friend of yours to have another coffee with you, give them a list of your RSQs, and talk to them about how you think your data provide answers to each of these RSQs. It can also be a good idea to switch on the voice recording function of your mobile phone so that really cogent bits of what you say and discuss can later be transcribed. Then go ahead and talk in detail about the answers to each of your research sub-questions, and importantly, as you go along, justify your answers with supporting data. Encourage your friend to ask questions of justification as you go along, and indeed any other supplementary questions which might help to make this more of a conversation than a monologue. Don't be afraid to stop and say to them – 'can I try again?' Like the Café questions, the rephrasing of an answer can, and usually does, increase its clarity and validity to both the listener and the speaker.

After the session, play back the conversation and note down any key points made in answer to each research sub-question. Particularly note any critical comments your friend may offer, such as the following:

That doesn't seem to follow from what you first said

or

What evidence do you actually have for that answer?

or

I'm not sure why you think your data allows you to challenge that view.

Importantly, also note the quality of your replies to these and reflect on whether they were good enough. By understanding the descriptions and justifications of your answers to the RSQs, you now also have the structural bones for this discussion chapter.

So now, create this structure by using your research subquestions as subheadings in the chapter, and then draft out how you have answered them. However, don't just provide answers to your empirical RSQs. Interweave into each discussion of these the appropriate information from the literature RSQs. You will then be in a position to show how your results contribute and provide new insights into the existing literature in your area. Remember though, whilst using such information from earlier literature chapters, do remain focused on the key issues of this discussion chapter – the answers to your final RSQs. In sum, keep focused on the answers to these RSQs, but use the answers to your literature RSQs to inform the synthesis you have gained.

When you have done this, you should be in a position to attempt an answer to your main research question. At this point then you should now be ready for the last chapter of your thesis.

The conclusions and recommendations chapter

Conclusions

Rather like the introductory chapter, this chapter should be clear and logical, as well as quite short. The first task is to go through the answers to all of your RSQs once more. You need to remind the reader of what you concluded about the RSQs in the last chapter, but only provide short summaries of these conclusions. Once again, be aware of the danger of too much repetition – you are only using repetition to remind the reader of what has been discussed and concluded, but this chapter's central purpose is to present a synthesis of the information contained in the answers to your RSQs to arrive at an answer to your MRQ.

To avoid such repetition, it is a good idea to re-read what you wrote in previous chapters about the answers to these RSQs, and then – without looking at what you said there – write new summaries of the answers to them. Once each summary is complete, it is a good idea to go back to previous chapters once more and add page numbers indicating where the data justifying these answers are located. This will be all the information your examiners should need here. By avoiding over-long repetition, your examiners will be given summaries of your findings which demonstrate your ability to condense these answers in such a manner that allows you to manipulate them into the final stage – the answering of your MRQ.

So when you have completed the summary answers to each of the RSQs, it's a good idea to now set up a time for a final question-and-answer session with your friend: this time a recorded conversation of the answer to your *main research question*. As this is likely to be your first attempt at a summation of what all the answers to the RSQs amount to, it will almost certainly need some repetition and clarification before you are happy with your answer. But once again, it makes sense to stand back from the evidence and to try and articulate what you think the answer actually is. Having gained a strong grasp of the answers to your RSQs by now, you should be able to turn all of these into an articulation of the answer to your MRQ. From here, and using the conversation recording as an aid, you should be able to turn this into a written answer.

So to summarize the process, please do the following:

- work out full replies to the answers to the relevant RSQs (literature, conceptual, and empirical RSQs); these go in the previous chapter;

- then produce summaries of these full replies and place them at the start of this chapter;

- then, first orally, and then on paper, synthesize these into an answer for your MRQ.

Now that you have reached this position, it is no bad thing to spell out in what ways the answer to your MRQ is original. You have probably pointed this out earlier in your thesis, when you described what were the gaps in the field or the questions that still needed answering. But here, in your concluding chapter, to say how your thesis is original – whether this be in terms of its contribution to knowledge in the field, its new theoretical insights, its contribution to a methodological approach or its implications for policy and practice – is then an important reminder to your reader of the major strengths and originality of your work.

Recommendations

A doctoral student is normally expected to make recommendations arising from their research. These are often aimed at a number of different audiences. They may be policy makers, fellow academics and perhaps practitioners in related professional disciplines. In addition, an examiner will expect to see some recommendations for further research, as one of the paradoxical hallmarks of a good piece of research is that it normally raises as many questions as it answers. Research you have conducted for your thesis will very likely suggest the need for other pieces of research, and therefore in many ways the end of your thesis is the beginning of the rest of your research career. It is useful to employ a table here to catalogue and justify your recommendations, because it forces you to list in one column what you think your recommendations actually are, and then in the other column to identify precisely where in your thesis you have evidence which supports the particular recommendation. The table might look something like this:

My recommendation	Evidence for this may be found here ...

When you have completed the left hand column, make sure you can complete the one on the right. Any recommendation for which you cannot supply evidence is not a recommendation, and only part of a wish list.

Finally, it is sensible to reflect on what you might have done differently if you had the opportunity of starting again, and what lessons you have learnt about research from working on and completing your viva. These need to be carefully drafted and redrafted because the same pitfalls lie in wait for the unwary as in making recommendations.

All done? Not quite: Twenty structural leaks to check for before you stop

Before you decide that it's time to stop and hand the thesis in, it's a very good idea to fully reflect on the major structural issues of your thesis, and consider their watertightness. Listed below, then, are twenty potential structural weaknesses, or 'leaks'. We've put these at the end of this chapter, but don't mean to imply that you should leave these until the end of your programme: if you're reading this book at the beginning or part-way through your doctorate, they are the sorts of questions that should be read and revisited from time to time, as your understanding of them develops. There are also some which you may not have met yet, but you would be wise to recognize that whilst you have not reached this stage of your thesis yet, you still might give some thought to the kinds of structural problems you are likely to encounter as you progress, and so begin to think ahead in how you might avoid them. Here then are twenty potential structural leaks with reasons for why they may be problems for your thesis:

1   **Are you the right person to research the subject of this thesis?** If your justification in insufficient, you probably won't have access to vital information needed to properly structure the thesis or provide doctoral level answers.

2   **Have you got the right title for your thesis?** If you have worded it wrongly (or haven't changed it as the thesis has changed), then it won't reflect the structure or the evidence within the thesis.

3   **Have you given, and will you continue to give, serious reflection to how you intend structuring your time whilst researching your thesis?** Failure to proactively attempt to structure academic, social, family and other demands may seriously impede the development of your thesis.

4   **Have you given, and will you continue to give, serious reflection to structuring appropriate academic activities into different time sections of the thesis?** Failure to do so may result in having insufficient time to complete your thesis in a balanced manner.

5   Have you given serious thought, and continue to do so, on how you spend the wordage in different chapters of the thesis? Failure to do so could lead to unbalanced chapters in an unbalanced thesis.

6   Does your introductory chapter succinctly explain your area of interest, the focus of your research, the MRQ, the subsequent RSQs and the linkage between the RSQs and the thesis chapters? This is the crucial structuring chapter, and failure to do this may seriously limit the development of the thesis.

7   Can you explain to a stranger, in under forty seconds, the focus of your research, the MRQ and how the subsequent RSQs are deconstructed from it? This is crucial to your justification of the structuring of your thesis, and failure to be able to do this confidently may seriously affect examiners' judgements of your control of the structure of your thesis.

8   Does the wording of your MRQ describe precisely what is tackled in the thesis? If you get this wrong, your structure won't reflect the central question of the thesis, nor the evidence used to answer it.

9   Is the number of RSQs exactly the number created by deconstructing the MRQ? If you get this wrong, your RSQs won't provide the exact evidence needed to answer your MRQ.

10 Does the wording of your RSQs precisely describe what each tackles in the thesis? If any of these are wrong, these RSQs won't provide the evidence needed to answer that part of the MRQ.

11 Have you identified literature/context/conceptual RSQs, a methodology RSQ and results RSQs? All of these are essential in structuring the thesis, and failure to identify them may cause serious structural problems.

12 Have you selected the appropriate literature/context/ conceptual reviews to properly investigate your MRQ? If you have selected the wrong ones or omitted one that should be there, then you may have supplied the wrong or insufficient information to fully understand the MRQ.

13 Have you explained how your literature/context/conceptual reviews inform your research findings? If you don't, you may miss the synergy between earlier material in the thesis and your research findings, and thus miss critical research insights and fail to explore them.

14 Have you got the right balance in the use of the tools of description, analysis and synthesis in your thesis? If you get this balance wrong, and particularly if there is insufficient analysis and synthesis, you may not have provided the quality of concepts and information required in a doctoral thesis.

15 Are the methods chosen appropriate to the kind of data required? If they are inappropriate, they will fail to yield the data needed to answer your MRQ, and undermine the whole doctoral process.

16 Have you justified the degree to which you think your findings can be classed as epistemologically 'objective'? Failure to do so may have serious repercussions on the nature of the claims you make for them.

17 Does the extent of the claims you make match the nature of your findings? If you over- or under-claim on your findings, then you demonstrate serious inconsistency in your thinking.

18 Does the extent of the claims you make match the nature of your sample? If you over- or under-claim on your findings from the nature of your sample, then you demonstrate a misunderstanding in the nature and purpose of sampling techniques.

19 Have you identified the originality of your findings or justified the contribution of the thesis to the literature? If you don't, you may fail to see the relationship between your research and the current status of your discipline, and thereby fail to structure in this significance.

20 Have you properly balanced the nature of your findings with the claims that you make for these findings? If you fail to do so, you may be accused of not understanding the nature of your findings.

The final page of the thesis

At the beginning of the book, we suggested that 'I' is not a word we favour in a doctorate. Call it old-fashioned if you like, but it's important to convey through your writing your ability to distance yourself and your feelings from the work you are engaging with. Too many 'I's can suggest (to us at least) that the candidate may be taking too personal a position. Be that as it may, we also suggested that at the start of a thesis that it's no bad thing to talk about who you are, why you're the right person to do this research, and why you want to do it – there's a story to be told of how you developed as a researcher, and this is one place to do it. The other place can be at the very end of the thesis, almost like an epilogue, where you talk about what you've learnt from the experience and what importance you attach to doing this work. We then want to finish with a last page by a successful doctoral candidate, Rob Kennett (Kennett, 2009), whose thesis was in large part concerned with better suicide prevention techniques for members of the police. Technically, this probably should have come before our '20 leaks' section. But we think this is a better finish. The page demonstrates very well the benefit that Rob gained from his doctoral journey.

> Finally, this journey has reminded me why I joined the service. I joined the service over 30 years ago to save life and uphold the law of this country. I have increasingly dedicated myself to saving lives through my skills in negotiation. I have saved many lives, but this study has provided me with a depth of understanding that has proved invaluable. I can state that as a direct result of using the knowledge gathered in this study I have saved two lives that before this journey I would have probably failed to do. In particular, I recall one young man on a ledge high above the ground. We talked and I realised that he had determined that this was the end. As we talked I remembered Strentz (2006) and focused on regret, because by taking his life, all other options, opportunities, and experiences would be removed. My research saved his life. For me undertaking this rigorous academic work has proved to be a worthy enterprise, for lives have been and will continue to be saved as a result of it.

PART THREE

Moving out

CHAPTER TEN

The examiners' need for structural clarity

Introduction: The importance of the examiner

We've mentioned throughout the thesis the importance of the views of the external examiner. They are not dragons. Most are thoughtful, diligent and rather nice people. However, you need to satisfy their requirements to achieve your doctorate, so they do play a crucial role. So understanding what they want to see in your thesis is critical to its success, and good structuring is very dear to their hearts, both because it not only demonstrates that you know what you are doing, but also makes life a lot easier for them. And the one thing you don't want to do in a thesis is upset your examiners.

Now early in our meetings with doctoral students, we usually provide them with something like the following story of a thesis examiner, before putting a couple of questions to them:

> Your examiner has been sent your thesis. They are already heavily committed with other work, and are going to have to space out the reading of your thesis over a number of days in order to deal with it and all the other demands. They know the academic area you are writing in well, but the truth is that they aren't

particularly motivated by your writing style. It's been raining all day, their feet are wet, it's half seven in the evening when they get home, and they are tired, and the evening meal has been too long in the oven. And they know they need to read a couple of chapters of your thesis tonight, when quite honestly, they'd rather curl up in front of the television, and watch their favourite series before going to bed.

The questions to our students then are the following:

- Given that they are going to read some of your thesis tonight, what kinds of things must you make sure you do NOT do in the thesis?

- And what should you always try to ensure that you WILL do in the thesis?

We covered a little of this in Chapter 3, but we want to go a little deeper here. As you work through your doctorate, you will inevitably make some mistakes – and hence our students will hear our warning at various times that 'if I was an external examiner and I read this …', because we have both been external examiners and we have a pretty good idea of what most will be thinking, as we've been in their shoes many times ourselves. And one thing we do know: if you make the work of reading your thesis difficult, they are not going to be happy.

The needs of the examiner: Three questions

Now it is no great revelation to begin by saying that you are not writing for yourself, you are writing for *your readers*, but it is surprising how often even experienced writers forget that unless you are writing a private diary, from the start you should be thinking of them and their needs as you are writing your thesis. A number of questions are important here.

A first one is the following:

- Are you making your writing clear and accessible?

Please read the following and ask yourself: how do you think your examiners would react to reading something like this:

> Indeed dialectical critical realism may be seen under the aspect of Foucauldian strategic reversal – of the unholy trinity of Parmenidean /Platonic Aristotelian provenance; of the Cartesian - Lockean - Humean - Kantean paradigm, of foundationalisms (in practice, fideistic foundationalisms) and irrrationalisms (in practice, capricious exercises of the will-to-power or some other ideologically and/or psychosomatically buried source) new and old alike; of the primordial failing of western philosophy, ontological monovalence, and its close ally, the epistemic fallacy with its ontic dual; of the analytic problematical laid down by Plato, which Hegel served only to replicate in his actualist monovalent analytic reinstatement in transfigurative reconciling dialectical connection, while in his hubristic claims for absolute idealism he inaugurated the Comtean, Kierkegaardian and Neitzschean eclipses of reason, replicating the fundaments of postivism through its transmutation route to the superidealism of a Baudrillard. (Bhaskar, 1996)

We personally get about three or four lines into this piece before we lose our way (and that's having had many attempts at reading it). We politely suggest that if you write in a jargon-infested, portentous, never-ending sentence kind of way, your supervisor might be kind enough to read it through and simply put next to it 'can you make this clearer please?'. Your examiner (especially if they have just waded their tired way through an unpalatable late meal) will likely put a pencil through it, mark it 'unreadable', and expect you to rewrite it as part of your referral (because that's the kind of formative judgement they will probably be moving towards). In countries where the viva is an important event, they may make a note of wanting you to explain it there. If you can do this, then they are still likely to want you to rewrite it; if you can't explain it, their judgement of you sinks lower and lower. And of course, they'll check to see if it's been plagiarized. And if there is not just one piece like this, but many of these kinds of sentences, your examiners won't ask you to explain each one; they'll probably put a line through all of them and ask for a major thesis rewrite.

So in this example, you've got a thesis examiner who doesn't like the fact that you haven't thought of his or her needs and who isn't sure exactly what you are saying and doesn't believe that this is because they are too stupid to understand what you are saying. That's a very dangerous position to get into as a doctoral candidate. So clarity and thinking of how you can help your reader to understand what you are saying are both essential qualities of any doctoral student's writing approach.

Now a second question follows from this. Thinking of your reader means more than writing clearly and carefully. It means gently reminding them of what has gone before. And again this goes back to knowing something about the life of the examiner. Some examiners may have little else to do but read your thesis. However, the majority, like our examiner above, are hard-worked, and because of other work commitments will likely plan to read your thesis over a number of days: a couple of chapters, perhaps, on Monday morning, Tuesday afternoon for a couple more, Thursday morning and Friday afternoon for the remainder of the thesis, and then Saturday morning for pulling their thoughts together, writing their preliminary report and if a viva is part of the examination rubric, deciding on the questions they want to ask during it.

Now, it will be clear that they have other tasks to deal with in between reading your chapters. So issues of remembering what has been read previously are likely to occur during the week. So the question here is the following:

- What can you do to help them remember what they have read previously?

Now you might do nothing: after all, you don't *have* to. But as we've said, your examiner is a busy person, and if they finish chapter 2 on Monday morning, for example, but then have lots of meetings and other reading to complete before they re-engage their mind with your thesis on Tuesday afternoon, they will have to remind themselves of what you have covered in chapters 1 and 2 before they begin chapter 3.

And you *can* make life easier for them. If at the start of chapter 3, you not only remind them of the central purpose of the thesis, and how chapters 1 and 2 have helped in this understanding, but go on to say that in chapter 3 (the chapter they are about to read), the following issue/Research Sub-Questions (RSQ) will be addressed, and this will help in answering *this* part of the Major Research Question (MRQ), and that you'll do this in the chapter by first looking at *a*, before examining *b* and *c*, before finally coming to *d*, you've done a number of really useful and helpful things for them such as the following:

i   you've reminded them of the central purpose of the thesis;

ii   you've reminded them of what chapters 1 and 2 were about and why they were important to the overall thesis;

iii   you've let them know at the start of chapter 3 why the subject matter of chapter 3 comes after the materials in chapters 1 and 2;

iv   you've let them know what questions the chapter will focus upon, why it will focus on them, and how the chapter is therefore structured.

In so doing, you've made the examiner's job that much easier, and they will probably say 'thank you' quietly, before they get down to read the rest of the chapter. If, however, you don't do these things and leave them to work out what it is they are reading and why they are reading it, well, we don't need to spell out how comparatively unhelpful this is, do we? Such lack of help will likely be taken as a sign by the examiner that this doctoral candidate hasn't had the reader in mind when they've written the chapter. And they may then come to your chapter a little more negatively minded – and probably to future chapters as well. It may also raise a suspicion in the examiner's mind that you haven't provided such an overview and such clarity because you don't know how to do these things. And that also will not be good for their overall judgement of your ability.

Train journey or mystery tour?

The next question then continues the same theme and asks you to stand back and think about your thesis as a whole. It's been raised earlier, but because it is so important it needs more reflection. It asks the following:

●   Is your thesis a train journey, where stops and destinations, and the reasons for them, are made clear to the reader; or is it a mystery tour, where the reader either has to do the work in making sense of the direction and intentions of your thesis, or simply waits for this understanding to appear?

Now some very good writing is based upon the mystery tour idea. Some of the best crime fiction is written in this way as the writer deliberately teases the reader, plotting in things like red herrings and laying down subtle clues as to who the murderer is. You as a reader may very well be attracted by this kind of approach, and you may have bought a crime novel either because you wanted to see if you could spot the murderer before the writer reveals all at the end, or to simply enjoy the way the writer is playing with you, as they try to place and manipulate assumptions.

However, we strongly advise that you do *not* use any of these approaches with your thesis. Your examiner is not reading your thesis for the entertainment of trying to guess the ending, nor of working out how you got there, nor of simply experiencing the pleasure of what you have written. A central part of their job is not only to gauge your ability as a writer and researcher and the manner in which you compile and deploy your evidence but also to see whether you have the ability to structure the arguments that make up the thesis. And if they are reading a thesis where the writer has left them to do this themselves, rather than it being demonstrated to them by the writer, then they are not only going to be unhappy about the extra work you have imposed on them but also going to be troubled about your writing ability.

A train journey, then, is a better metaphor for the journey of structuring and writing a thesis, because it suggests a number of useful things a writer should be doing. It suggests the following:

- You, the writer, should have a very clear overview of the journey as a whole.

- You should know the destination of the thesis and understand why this is the right destination for the thesis.

- You should know where you need to stop along the journey in order to gather the materials which ensure that you arrive at the correct destination.

- You should be aware that your reader needs to know these things as well.

The reader should then be left in no doubt that you, the writer, are sufficiently clear to be able to communicate all of these to them throughout the thesis.

For the examiner, then, the ability to do these things well tells them that you, the writer, are aware of your own reasoning, how and why you are planning your journey, and how and why all these stops contribute to the final destination. Very importantly, it provides the map by which the examiners can judge how well you perform on the journey itself. Your clarity of thinking, and the structure that comes from this, enable them to judge the quality of your thesis far more easily – and it gives them confidence in you.

Travelling on the wrong track

These actions will be really helpful to you in avoiding or correcting a very common mistake that happens along many a doctoral journey. This is the temptation to take a branch railway line away from the main line track. In doctoral thesis parlance, it means to be distracted by a lesser thesis issue and to focus on material which doesn't help you answer your MRQ. Most researchers have done this: we have a topic we want to address and begin reading on it. No problem so far. But then we become so interested in one particular facet that that aspect begins to consume us. We read everything we can find about it, but in the process we begin to lose our focus and to neglect the other parts we should be reading about. In so doing, we begin to not only lose the overall balance of the research with which we are engaged but also forget what we are aiming to do in the thesis.

Now occasionally, this new interest can legitimately change the entire direction of the research. After all, if you have stumbled across something which throws up new insights, which suggests new experimentation and whose promise doesn't diminish no matter how critical you try to be, then you may well be on to something of considerable importance. But this change of direction will require considerable reflection, and discussion with colleagues and supervisors on the implications of such a course of action, not least because if you do decide to follow this track, a great deal of the rest of the thesis will probably need to be changed to accommodate this new focus and direction.

Unfortunately, however, on many occasions, a side-track/branch line is precisely that – a dead end that takes up valuable time, and out of which you need to reverse to link up with the main line track again. This can be very wasteful of time and energy, particularly in an age when you, your supervisors and probably your funding body have limits to the length of time that can be spent researching and writing the thesis.

So you need to be really clear about the alternatives in front of you, and in many cases, the best advice is 'when in doubt, don't.' And being really clear on what you are doing and why you are doing it is then not only helpful to your examiner, it can also be immensely helpful to you as well: you are much more likely to recognize if you are heading off down dead ends, if you are clear and can vocalize what your final destination is, and what is needed to get there, and can compare this destination with the one to which this new route will take you.

Linear and non-linear travel on a thesis journey

However, it's important to recognize that though a railway journey is a good metaphor, it's not perfect. At the start of the thesis you may plan out your MRQ, Thesis Title, RSQs and Chapter headings and foci, in what may look like a linear set of tasks, yet the reality of the journey's challenge is often very different. The literature reviews you undertake may throw up issues that you hadn't considered previously and require some adjustment to your RSQs, and perhaps to the MRQ. Then the creation of an appropriate framework for investigating your MRQ may change. As noted earlier, the UK descriptors for doctoral work (QAA, 2014) state that the doctoral student must possess not only

> the general ability to conceptualise, design and implement a project for the generation of new knowledge, applications or understanding at the forefront of the discipline

but also, if the unexpected happens,

to adjust the project design in the light of unforeseen problems. (our italics)

The thesis ending then may change as you progress through the RSQs and the chapters, and, as you progress, some stops you hadn't anticipated may well be needed. Whilst the final document will likely be framed and written as an essentially linear journey, its reality is much more complicated, as reflection and iteration are always essential ingredients. This is why we have said more than once that the introduction is usually just about the last thing you write: so much has changed since you started, that the initial introduction may no longer properly reflect the journey that has been undertaken.

But such iteration is very different from having little idea of where your doctorate will end up and what you need to do to get there. Your examiners will understand the need for such adjustments, and you shouldn't be afraid to acknowledge such changes as the thesis progresses. Growth, iteration and change are very common in research (despite what the final versions of many published academic papers may suggest), and any examiner worth their salt will want to see your growth in this area – as this will be one of the key criteria by which they judge if you have developed and grown as a researcher during the process.

So as supervisors, we're always trying to encourage such development. Indeed, we're always trying to wear at least two hats: the supervisor's, who should be a critical support and adviser, and the examiner's, who is essentially working out if this thesis should ultimately pass or fail. Hence the reason why quite a lot of our feedback to students takes the form of 'if I were the examiner of this thesis, I would probably say …'. As examiners, we would want the candidate to provide us with a clear road map or train timetable explaining what they are doing, where they are going, why they are going where they are going and how they are going to get there.

If then you keep in mind the wants and needs of your examiner, you will be preparing a more persuasive thesis, and if you have to go through a summative viva, you will be that much more prepared. That is the subject of the next chapter.

CHAPTER ELEVEN

Preparing for the summative viva

Introduction

There are some countries in which summative vivas are not held, and doctoral candidates in these countries may then think there is little need to read this chapter. But if you are reading this book either near the beginning of your thesis or a little way in, then this chapter can still be of considerable use, even if you have no final viva to face. Like discussions on formative vivas, examinations and the role and nature of the examiner, an early discussion of summative vivas is useful to any doctoral candidate, as it is another way of helping the candidate to understand the major issues with which an examiner is concerned. So, whether examiners judge a thesis by the written thesis alone, by assignments, written thesis and summative viva or by written thesis and summative viva, this chapter helps ensure that all bases are well covered.

What is a viva?

Technically, the full term is the Latin *viva voce*, which literally means 'with living voice'. It is often translated as 'by word of mouth', and refers to a final oral examination conducted by examiners after a thesis has been submitted. Depending on the country and the university, it can take place in a public setting, in a university room where a group of individuals may ask questions or in a smaller university room where student, examiners and normally a chair, as well as a supervisor, meet. But size, shape and variety do not alter a viva's ultimate purposes: to demonstrate to other scholars that the candidate has written and understood the thesis, to clarify any points of misunderstanding, to see if candidates can justify the decisions they have taken on things like thesis structuring and to defend it against any criticisms examiners may level at it. A viva then involves many of the skills used in writing the thesis, but it also requires the oral and social skills of interacting with others in presenting and defending a coherent argument. Some in favour of the use of a viva would also suggest that if students are to be awarded such a prestigious degree, they need to be able to demonstrate their worth not just through the written word but through oral justification as well.

The normal structure of a summative viva

Once again, there are cultural variations here, but normally viva structure consists of formal introductions, a brief description of the conduct of the session to the student, housekeeping issues (tea, coffee, allowances for comfort breaks etc.), and then movement into a question-and-answer session. This usually begins with gentle introductory questions (*Why did you decide to research in this area? What have you personally gained from doing a doctorate?*) before moving to a series of questions which are shared between examiners, beginning, unsurprisingly, with the introductory chapters. Literature and methodological chapters are then worked through, before questions are asked about the conduct of the research, and then questions on the results and the conclusions drawn. Finally, discussion is usually had of the recommendations and future research in the area.

   The questions then tend to follow the direction of the thesis structure, though how long examiners spend on each section will depend on what they think is problematic and needs further explanation. They are also likely to ask questions on areas that particularly interest them. You may have already quoted them in your thesis and so know where they are 'coming from', but if not, it may be useful to do a little research before the viva on *their* background to have an idea of their interests.

Now when the questions have been asked, you will normally be asked if you have anything you want to say, anything you want to clarify further to the answers you gave in the viva and whether there are any questions you want to ask the examiners. When all this is complete, you will be asked to leave the room, and the examiners will begin to make their decision.

That is the standard structure, and we'll return to the decision process later in this chapter, but let's return to the period before the viva begins and look at the role that formative vivas can play and consider the kind of questions which might be asked there.

Formative vivas

Now we've mentioned throughout this book how many university regulations require examinations and judgements during the programme, and how they work like formative vivas, as they help you to reflect on what you are doing well, and where you are struggling and need to put in more work, and perhaps ask for advice. The confirmation review, usually held at the end of the first year, is excellent for this, as it is common for a number of things to be requested: a written piece, an overview of the thesis structure, and a plan for moving forward. From the questions asked at such exercises you should become more aware of where you are doing well, what further work needs doing, and what challenges you are likely to meet ahead. So many of the formal and informal sessions you experience throughout your programme can act as formative vivas, from which you can learn a great deal.

'Viva roulette'

But don't wait until near your summative viva before trying to phrase and answer such questions. One exercise we use with groups of students is called 'viva roulette'. The game is very simple and works for students at all stages of their programme. Basically, we ask three or four students to sit together at a table, and a pack of cards is placed in front of them, face down. We ask one of them to shuffle the cards, and then ask that another takes the top card, turns it over and reads what is written on it to the rest of the group. As we explain, on each card is written a typical viva question, and they must do their best to answer the question, whilst their colleagues at the table listen to the answer, and ask supplementary questions of clarification or extension. As you will see in Box 11.1, the questions tend to follow a standard thesis structure. This means that most students coming to the end of their first year should be able to answer with some comfort questions on the Major Research Question and Research Sub-Questions, the thesis structure, literature reviews, the emerging methodology and any proposed research methods. If, however, the question asked on the card is one to which, as yet, the candidate does not possess the information, then they simply place the card at the bottom of the pack, and turn over another for a more appropriate question. The value of this exercise lies not just in the oral explanation of answers, which can help a person better understand what they are thinking; it also provides a safe environment within which to practise answers to typical viva questions, as well as to any follow-up questions. Finally, it allows students to practice (and to listen to others practice) answers at different stages in their doctoral journey, and to reflect on how their answers change as they progress.

Box 11.1: Viva roulette questions

- Why did you decide to research in this area?
- What have you personally gained from doing the research?
- What is your main research question, and why did you select it?
- What is the argument of your thesis?
- In what ways is your thesis original, and how does it contribute to the body of knowledge in the area?
- Are there cultural aspects of your research which make it distinctive?

Box 11.1: (Continued)

- Which particular contexts add to the originality of your findings?

- What have been the most striking/surprising things in your literature reviews?

- How did your literature reviews inform your research questions?

- Why did you use the research techniques you adopted?

- How did you establish their reliability or their trustworthiness?

- What do you see as the strengths and limitations of your findings?

- If you could go back in time, which aspects of your research would you do differently?

- Do you think your positionality has affected your research?

- What aspects of your research do you believe are publishable, and why?

- What recommendations do you think can be extracted from your findings for policy makers?

- What avenues for further research do you consider your research has opened up?

Now these questions are only, and can only be, general viva questions. They are not, and cannot be, the kind of questions specific to an individual thesis, and to a particular discipline. These more specific kinds of questions usually begin something like the following:

> Would you please turn to p. 53 in your thesis. On that page, you state that … . So why … ?

Or

> How did your positionality as a medical consultant impact upon your approach to the research … ?

Mock vivas

We also arrange 'mock vivas' with our students once the thesis is complete and submitted, as this is a period of time where preparations can be made for the summative viva. So perhaps a week, or a few days before the real thing happens, we carry out this 'mock' viva. Whilst some may have reservations about these, particularly if the student is of a nervous disposition, we still feel that they are very useful if handled sensitively. We'll briefly describe how we conduct ours to give you a flavour of what you might personally experience.

We normally begin by simply walking the student through the format of the viva – where it will be held, its structure, the role of the chairperson and examiners, and the supervisor's role (we'll come to all of this in a couple of pages). If we can, we take them into the room in which the real viva will take place: it sounds a minor thing, but it's also new information they won't need to process on the day, and a supervisor should ensure that a student goes into their viva concerned only about the questions they have to answer.

Now some days before the mock viva, the student will have been given the viva roulette questions for them to reflect upon. They will also have been told that some of these will be included in the mock viva. But at the mock viva itself, we also intersperse questions specific to the student's thesis, issues that we've discussed previously, and which we think may come up in the viva proper, and which it therefore would be useful for them to practise. We also put in one or two 'tricky' questions so that they can reflect on how they would best deal with any like these at the real viva.

We tell them that during this mock viva, we'll go into examiner mode and act and ask questions like an examiner. However, we also reassure them that if they stumble on a question, don't know how to reply to one, or if there are other issues we think it important to comment upon at that moment, and not at the end of the exercise, we tell the student that we'll come out of external examiner mode and will discuss with them whatever the issue is. Then, when we feel the student is sufficiently comfortable with the agreed resolution, we go back into examiner mode and try again. And when we've gone through all the questions we want to ask (probably about forty-five minutes' worth), we stop and have a general discussion with them about the process, in which the student can ask any questions they want to. In very exceptional circumstances, we may suggest (or the student may ask for) another mock viva. Here, a judgement has to be made on whether such an addition would make them less, rather than more confident in preparing for the viva proper. The feedback from our students on such mock vivas suggests that they find the exercise demanding but extremely helpful and a really good preparation for the summative viva.

Dealing with tricky questions

As noted earlier we always include one or two tricky questions, because if a student hasn't encountered this type before the summative viva, they may be thrown by them so much that it can affect the rest of their performance in the viva. These are ones we think students need to be aware of and discuss beforehand, and here we suggest two which students can have difficulties with.

a   *What is the argument of your thesis?* Even though this is not an easy question, it is often an early question in the viva, because it asks the student to reflect upon the overall thesis project. Yet even for the experienced student, it can be quite difficult to answer. It is asking more than simply 'what is your thesis about?', and the following answers are insufficient as replies:

- My thesis is about doctors' interactions with nurses in the treatment of terminally ill patients.
- My thesis is about the extinction of Denisovan man.
- My thesis is about non-directive counselling.

Instead, the question is looking for a candidate's ability to describe how the focus and evidence of the thesis impacts and develops their chosen area of research. So better responses would be as follows:

- The thesis is arguing that the data gathered in context w, suggest that doctors and nurses bring different professional perspectives to the treatment of terminally ill patients, and treatment would be much better if both were more aware of these different perspectives through the provision of targeted training.

- The thesis is arguing that the data gathered in context m with techniques l, m, and n suggest that Denisovan man died out during a series of climatic events, and that these played the role of weakening existing members such that other factors, particularly competition from Homo sapiens, eventually led to their extinction.

- My data gained in context y suggest that much non-directive counselling is actually highly directive, but in an unvoiced and largely unconscious manner, and this realization needs to be an essential part of consciousness raising in the training of counsellors.

Exercise: so, now, can you state what you think the argument of your thesis is? To help you, here are five incomplete sentences, elements of which you may incorporate into your answer:

- Much of the evidence in the literature I have reviewed suggests_____.

- The problem I'm interested in has been neglected because_____.

- So by using the following techniques_____.

- I have gathered/want to gather evidence which will help me determine/suggests that_____.

- This will impact on the area of practice by_____.

Save what you write for reflection and integration into a reply on this question.

  b A second question which, if asked, normally comes towards the end of the viva is, *if you could go back in time, which aspects of your research would you do differently?* Now advice on your final chapters has suggested that this kind of reflections should be included in your thesis. But if you didn't include some reflection there, then there is a real danger that the question may be answered before full thought is given to it, and you may say things which don't help your cause. So stop, take a breath, and ask one of the following questions:

- I'm sorry, could you repeat that question?
- I'm not sure I understand; can you rephrase what you are asking?
- When you ask that question, do you mean … ?

Asking for a repeat or rephrasing of the question does two things: it can help you better comprehend what is being asked, and it can also provide valuable time for you to reflect upon what might be meant here, providing sufficient delay to think about how much should be said. If you give some thought to this question, you are likely to come to the following conclusions:

- This is a good thesis which doesn't have any really major problems.
- The examiners expect *something* – if only to demonstrate my reflexivity and self-criticality.
- So what aspect of the thesis could have been improved in a perfect world, but doesn't suggest that the thesis is a poor one? Some of these might be:
  - an aspect of a literature or policy approach which could have been developed slightly more;
  - the use of an extra (but relatively minor) method to throw further light on already triangulated findings;
  - the inclusion of a stakeholder group in addition to those interviewed.

If your supervisors don't raise this question with you at the mock viva, it's a good thing to have a discussion on.

One final issue: what if, shortly before your viva, you notice that there is an element of the thesis you *know* is incorrect? What should you do? Once again, it is assumed that you have worked hard at your thesis, and so feel confident about your work overall. The mistake is then likely to be something relatively minor. What do you do: admit it or try to defend it as best you can? Our view is simply to admit it: defending what is indefensible will not put you in a good light with your examiners. One of us has experienced this situation. Before his viva, he was re-reading his thesis for the umpteenth time and spotted a clear logical mistake. He thought about this, and then decided, if it was raised at the viva, to admit to it. And of course it was: 'Now please turn to page 128, where you have written … .' The look of disappointment on the examiner's face when the mistake was immediately admitted was a pleasure to see and cost only a very minor correction by the author.

The role of the chair, the examiners and supervisors during the viva process

So now we've dealt with tricky issues, let's move to the viva proper. Once again, there is much cultural variation in the roles of the different players in the viva process.

By and large *the chairperson* (if there is one) is there to see that fair play is done. They don't normally read the thesis, but will usually explain the viva format to the student; they make sure that the viva runs in this manner, and will rule if they feel the boundaries are being abused. In our experience, a chairperson's intervention is very infrequent, but where it occurs, it can be a valuable form of action. They also keep aware of the comfort needs of the candidate, and perhaps most importantly should keep detailed notes on the questions asked and replies given, so that they can provide a neutral and authoritative source if there is a complaint about the conduct of the viva or the decision taken, later down the line.

We've talked a great deal in this book about *the examiners*, and in terms of actual viva conduct, they will normally have produced independent reports of the thesis and then met just before the viva and exchanged views on the quality of the thesis, and what they personally would like to explore within it. They will therefore have discussed the questions they want to ask and will usually divide these up, which means that one of them asks a number of questions before the other(s) takes over and asks some of their own.

And what of *the supervisor*? What do they do during the viva? Well, this can vary from culture to culture. In some cases the candidate has the right to decide if their supervisors attend or not, and if such an invitation is possible, it's usually a good idea to have them present, for the support prior to and during the viva and during the time before the decision is announced. When the candidate is told of the decision, they are normally very tired, and details of the feedback can then be missed, misunderstood or forgotten. The supervisor, who most times will have been through this process before, can provide the student with the knowledge of what will happen, and a much better record of what has gone on. Certainly, when we are talking about the viva process with our students, we tell them that we normally remain silent throughout, but will be taking copious notes on what is being asked, and on the replies they give, to enable us to gain a sense of how we think the examiners are reacting not only to individual replies, but also to the student's overall performance.

After the examiners' questions are complete, *the candidate* may be invited to repeat any answers they feel they didn't do particularly well on the first round. Then they may be invited to ask any questions themselves. Unless there is something really vital they want to say, we advise them to decline this offer. So, when the student has nothing else they want to say, the chair normally asks the student and the supervisor to leave the room, and to wait in another whilst a post-viva discussion is held between examiners and chairperson.

Post-viva discussions and the possible results

The chair will have listened carefully to the discussions, and they will be aware of and have the documentation describing the possible decisions that can be reached. Their job will then be to try to find agreement between the examiners on ticking the same box. This is not always straightforward; whilst some teams of examiners demonstrate close harmony in their judgements, this cannot be guaranteed, and there may be differences on the importance given to the student's performance in the summative viva, as well as on how satisfactorily the student performed. Such judgements then have to be combined with the judgements made on the thesis itself. Understandably, whilst the student may anxiously note that some time has gone since they left the examination room, the chair and examiners are necessarily taking their time in arriving at the final joint decision. *A very quick decision* usually means one of three things:

- The examiners think the thesis and the viva performance were so awful that the thesis has to be failed outright; this is very, very unusual, and if the student has performed creditably throughout their program, and worked well with their supervisors, this can be almost completely discounted.

- The examiners think the thesis and the viva performance were so outstanding that the thesis can be passed without any corrections. This isn't quite as unusual as an outright fail, but it *is* unusual: examiners normally like to show, even with the best of theses, that they have read them thoroughly and will normally note a few grammatical and spelling mistakes that need correcting. But straight passes do happen.

- The examiners thought very much the same about the written thesis, they agreed on the quality of the viva performance, and they agree that these two elements strongly suggest only one judgement. This happens, but even then, it normally takes a little time for such agreement to be reached.

The other judgements possible, besides a complete fail, or a complete pass, are phrased differently in different countries, but usually amount to the following:

- This is a very good thesis, but it has some minor corrections that need making, and these need sorting out before the degree is awarded; this amounts to a referral of perhaps only a few weeks.

- This is a good thesis, but there are a number of issues which needed clarifying, or expanding upon, and this amounts to a referral of a few months.

- This is a decent thesis, but there are a number of issues of clarification and expansion, and perhaps a small number of issues which haven't been addressed at all and need to be before the thesis is accepted, and this amounts to a referral of perhaps four to six months.

- This has the potential to be an acceptable thesis, but it has some substantial problems: besides issues of clarification and expansion and the reading of extra material, the student may need to re-examine the data, or even go and collect further data; this amounts to a referral of perhaps twelve months and the possibility of another viva when this is done.

- This does not meet the standard of a doctoral thesis, nor does it merit a fail; either it should be awarded a master's degree or only after stipulated corrections should it then be awarded a master's degree.

- The examiners cannot agree on a final verdict; this again is very unusual, but may require the appointment of new examiners, and the whole process be gone through again.

When the decision is agreed, student and supervisor are normally invited back into the examination room to be told the result: sometimes by the chair, sometimes by the external examiner, sometimes by the internal examiner. As well as the decision, normally brief reasons for it are given, and suggestions of what corrections need to be performed are suggested. Our experience is that for the student, apart from the actual result, the rest tends to be a bit of a blur: they probably haven't slept well the night before, they've used up much nervous energy at the viva, and had to think in such a tightly disciplined manner for so long, that they are usually too tired to take in all the details. Don't worry: the supervisor can listen, and sometimes ask on behalf of the student some points of clarification. In addition to such oral feedback, within a few days a jointly written statement by the examiners will be sent to the student, detailing the judgement, its reasons and the changes that still need to be made.

Dealing with the changes

As supervisors, we've never seen our role as ending with the viva. Like the student, we await the written report. When we've seen it and had time to read and digest it, we arrange to meet the student. At this meeting, we normally suggest that the response to the examiners needs dividing up into a number of stages:

i   First both supervisor and student need to read the report and requests very closely. If there are any doubts about precise meanings, then these need to be referred back to the examiners for clarification. This is crucial; there must be no ambiguity over what is required. The logic is simply this: if all are agreed on what is required, and if the things required are performed correctly, then the degree must be awarded. Any possibility that an examiner could come back after the revisions are submitted, and say, 'No, I didn't mean x, I meant y', or 'I should have added that you need to do ...' should be dealt with at this very early stage.

ii When the report has been closely analysed, the student should divide the report into the things that now need to be done. Usually, the report does this, but not always, and so the student needs to provide himself or herself with a complete list of all the individual bits which need doing.

iii We suggest to the student that they set up a table like Table 11.1, with an opening section on the issues in the report that need addressing; a description in the middle section on how these have been addressed; and the final section which indicates upon which page(s) an issue has been addressed.

TABLE 11.1 Table of thesis amendments

Issues needing addressing	How addressed	Pages on which issue is addressed
Issue 1		
Issue 2		
Issue 3		
Issue 4		

We strongly advise the first section to be filled in with the precise words that the report uses, and that the student does not attempt to provide an interpretation of them. The second section then should give a full description of the approach used in attending to them; and the final section should note all the pages on which the problem was tackled.

iv   We then suggest that as the issues are addressed on a particular page, the candidate should highlight in a bold colour (we like yellow) the changes/amendments/additions which have been made, so that the examiners can easily locate and read these.

v   As supervisors, we normally read not only the student's analysis of what needs doing, and the changes they make in accordance with this, but also the pages before and after these changes, to get a sense of how these changes impact on the text in the surrounding pages.

vi   Further, if, when the changes are being read, there is still some doubt in either the student's or the supervisor's mind as to whether the request for changes is really understood, then it is highly advisable to go back to one of the examiners (normally one of the internal examiners) to ensure that the approach does address what is requested.

vii   If all such issues are then resolved, the supervisors have read the table and agreed that the approach taken and the content used to resolve the issue are appropriate, then it is a good idea for the highlighting of all the changes made throughout the thesis to be retained, and a copy of the thesis with such highlighting be sent to the examiner(s), along with a copy of the table of thesis amendments. The examiners are then aided and guided in understanding what has been done and can easily locate where the changes have been made.

If such an approach is performed clearly, carefully and rigorously, the report on the thesis should come back fairly quickly, and with a positive response. And then it's time for some real celebrations: you have just gained your doctorate!

* * *

Now we originally thought to finish the book at this stage. But this third section is entitled 'Moving Out', and once the celebrations are over (or indeed sometimes before they are even engaged with) the aspiring academic will want to make more of their doctorate than just the degree. It is clearly a rich mine of material from which to write a number of important articles, and the process here is rather different from that of writing a doctorate. So our final chapter to this book is one providing advice on structuring and publishing your first articles. It is to this that we now turn.

CHAPTER TWELVE

Structuring and publishing your first articles

Introduction

We suggested at the end of the previous chapter that a book on structuring doctorates perhaps shouldn't finish with the success of the thesis, but rather with suggestions on how to get its research published elsewhere. And as articles can be published during your doctorate and can be harvested immediately after doctoral completion, the focus of this chapter is therefore on structuring and publishing peer-reviewed academic articles from it. It is also worth pointing out that if the intention from the beginning is to try to achieve the thesis through presenting a number of already published papers (and normally a connective piece), then this chapter will be extremely useful for such purposes.

It's now common practice for supervisors to point out to doctoral students that they should think actively about trying to get published a particularly good doctoral chapter or excellent essays from the taught element of a professional doctorate. Indeed, the assessment criteria of many universities now contain a section on whether doctoral pieces are worthy of publication, and if not, what needs to be done to make them so. Many supervisors then read chapters of doctoral theses with this question in mind. This seems excellent practice: the doctorate is, for many students, but a stepping-stone to greater things, and publication in an academic journal provides persuasive evidence of a student's suitability for appointment. We should also add that if material, suitably altered from a chapter or essay, *is* published, or is accepted for publication before the final examination of the thesis, it is perfectly acceptable (indeed, it is advisable) to quote this published piece in the thesis. In this way examiners know that readers from blind peer-reviewed international journals have already decided on the quality of the student's work. It's not a bad hint to give an examiner!

Articles, like doctorates, should be of high academic standard, but they do differ in some respects. One is more like acquiring the skills to climb a mountain; the other is more like writing a short story for a selective journal.

The doctorate is your academic learning experience, the way you learn your trade. Undergraduate essays may be viewed as the foothills in which you learn the initial skills of climbing academic mountains; masters' degrees take you as far as base camp, but it's only by going from base camp to the top of the mountain that you really come to grips with doctoral challenges. And once you've gained the expertise of such climbing, repeated experience through doctoral supervision builds up a core of 'tacit' knowledge (Polanyi, 1958) and understanding which help you see where others may be going wrong, and how you might help them. You then move from being a climber to becoming a guide and supervisor, and perhaps later to a doctoral examiner.

Articles are rather different beasts. Learning to write an article is essentially learning to write a short story for a selective journal. Whilst most doctorates normally have the length of a book (anywhere between 30,000 and 100,000 words), articles, irrespective of discipline, have much reduced lengths, which require the deployment of rather different skills to be written successfully. Crucial to such writing are four qualities: *hook*, *selection*, *focus* and *parsimony*.

So, we begin with the *hook*, and by this we mean 'how do you entice the reader to start and keep reading?' Your first readers are going to be the journal editor (who may only read the abstract) and the referees (who will read both abstract and article). They want to know three things from the start:

1 How does this article contribute to the discipline?
2 How does it contribute to the journal? and
3 Will this be done in an engaging manner?

Readers are unlikely to separate these three things out as they read: they want a question to be posed in an interesting manner which impacts not only on the discipline but on the nature of the journal, and they want it done in a readable manner. You, the writer, have to frame the beginning of the article so that it does all three things. You need to show from the start that there is a significant problem which needs resolving, that you will show how the problem can be answered, and what implications this has for the field. You then have to explain in the first few hundred words the problem and the solution in such a way that the reader is hooked into reading through to the end.

One of the best ways of doing this is to write the abstract and show it to colleagues. If they say 'Yes, I'd really like to read this, because …' then you're on the right lines. If you don't manage to generate any enthusiasm for what you have written, then you need to try again.

After the hook, but still intrinsic to it, comes the *selection*, for whilst a doctorate may have a number of 'gems' within it which could be turned into articles, not all can be squeezed into one publication. Three fairly standard ones are as follows:

- an article using a doctoral literature review to argue that an issue in the field hasn't been looked at in a particular way, and that this article will do this;

- an article using some of the doctorate's empirical data to demonstrate how it throws new light on a particular academic concern in the field;

- an article demonstrating how the doctoral findings have important implications for wider policy concerns in the field.

The differences don't want pushing too far, however: the structure taken in the article is likely to be similar to that taken in writing chapters in the doctorate. *Literature review/background/contextual articles* then are likely to be taken from individual doctoral chapters, which select and critique major viewpoints in the field and then show how their analyses reveal different ways of viewing issues. *Empirically based articles*, on the other hand, are likely to show how the mistakes or gaps in current research are addressed by the doctoral results.

Focus: Articles are then likely to follow the same structural logic as that practiced in the doctorate. But they will need to *focus down* to one particular aspect within the doctorate, whether this is a literature review, implications from selected doctoral results or questions raised for policies beyond the doctorate. However, the empirical results of an article cannot normally be used without the research context being supplied. Yet the article focus will still need to be the impact of these results, not on how this context impacts. In other words, the writer needs to decide upon what to focus and must ensure their article is oriented to this focus.

Parsimony: The writer also needs to be extremely *parsimonious* in the words used to write sections of the article. With a doctorate of 100,000 words, for instance, a wide exploration of issues is permitted; with 50,000 words there is much less luxury, which is why shorter doctoral theses can sometimes be harder to write than longer ones. With articles of much shorter length, there really isn't much space at all. The parsimonious choice of words and phrases to maintain brevity is going to be your watchword.

Getting the article structure right

Writing an article needs at least as much structuring as a chapter in your doctorate. We've already suggested that when writing doctoral chapters, it's not advisable to start writing and see where you end up. The same applies to writing articles. We know people who *can* write like this, but they tend to be masters of their art, and who, like the master teacher, or the chess grandmaster, have such deep understanding of the structure of their craft that their actions and decisions seem almost intuitive. They have an abundance of Polanyi's (1958) 'tacit knowledge' mentioned earlier. To the observer, they seem able to jump off a cliff and fly. We *don't* advocate this approach to those writers who are beginners: the beaches below those who try to fly too soon are littered with their rejected articles. Instead, and unsurprisingly, we advocate the kind of train journeys we have argued for throughout this book. In terms of the article or chapter, the key words to begin the piece will almost inevitably be as follows:

'In this article, I will ...' or 'This article argues that ...'

If you begin like this, you begin to commit yourself to

- letting the reader know what you intend to do;
- providing them with an order for this;
- sticking to that order throughout the article.

If you do this properly, the thought prior to actual writing may be nearly as long as that taken for writing the article itself. You then need to

- say in the opening paragraph what you intend to do and explain why and how the material and arguments within your article contribute to the corpus of knowledge in your disciplinary area;
- explain why your methodology is appropriate to produce the findings you need;
- demonstrate how your findings reach the conclusions suggested in your introductory paragraph.

Later in your career, you may be sufficiently capable to order the paper's argument in your head, or be able to write an opening paragraph and then subtly direct the rest of your writing onto these disguised train tracks, which in most cases are actually improved artistic expressions of the structures you use when you first start out. But it's a very risky business to begin like this.

Working on your writing processes

So you need to be clear about both argument and structure before you begin. But you also need to reflect upon how you are going to actually write this article. We've already seen that the article writing process, with its greater need for an immediate hook, its greater selectivity, focus and parsimony, is framed rather differently from the writing of doctoral chapters. Nevertheless, they do contain some similar issues, and one of the more obvious is the nature of the personal writing process.

Now different people have different levels of difficulty in writing. At one end of the spectrum, there are those who seem to write almost without effort, and produce first drafts which look remarkably like final ones. Unfortunately, however, such individuals tend to be the exceptions. Some people at the other end of the spectrum find the act of writing very stressful, and regard a period of sustained writing as equivalent to root canal surgery. Most people, however, would probably locate themselves somewhere between these two extremes – finding it hard work at times, but managing to get through the process to produce the first full draft, and then feeling rather good at this accomplishment.

A second thing to say is that there is one approach to writing which we wouldn't advise; that involves trying to force yourself to write. It's much better, we think, to go *round* the problem rather than *through* it. And people develop all kinds of strategies to do this:

- rewarding yourself – *if I write a thousand words I can have a coffee; I can have lunch; I can order that music …* ;

- fooling yourself – *begin a day's work by the comparatively easy task of editing the previous day's output, so that the semi-mechanical task of altering small phraseology flows into the next creative part*;

- dialoguing with the computer – *arguing with yourself about the argument or structure of what you are writing*;

- orally describing the next part – *walking up and down and explaining to yourself what you intend to do (and perhaps recording this monologue)*;

- turning the section to be written into a PowerPoint presentation – *and then transcribing the slides you create into a written format*.

You probably have other personal strategies, but whichever work for you, use and develop them. As Guccione and Wellington (2017, p. 45) said of thesis writing: 'What's the best motivator … the one that works for you.' The same applies to the writing of articles.

Selecting and engaging with the journal

Now in selecting a journal, you need to consider what quality of academic journal you initially want to aim for. Normally, the higher the quality of the journal, the more likely the rejection of your work, and if successful, probably the longer the time lag before it goes into print (though online publication eases that concern). On the plus side, all good academic journals are blind peer-reviewed, which means that the referees should not know a writer's identity, and so a relatively low academic status should not be part of any judgement of the article.

You would also be wise to do some homework on the journals you're aiming for. Journal editors are usually very pleased when a topic chosen by a writer becomes a theme that others pick up and write about as well; this gives a nice sense of continuity and development to the journal. So it's a good idea to go back about three or four years and look at the kinds of articles that have been published in it, and ask yourself questions like the following:

- Are they predominantly qualitative, quantitative or theoretic in orientation?
- Is there a particular school or thought to which it subscribes?
- Are the articles nationally or internationally focused?
- Does the journal specialize in particular issues within the field?

When you've got a 'feel' for the journal, reflect on how well you think your article would fit the journal's concerns. If the article seems to fit well, then you've probably found a good location for your work. If it means radically changing your focus and argument, and the article is therefore becoming distorted through being fitted into the journal culture, then perhaps another home is needed.

If you are unsure about any of these issues, then an email, or, better, a phone call to the editor is a good idea. They will not only help clarify your concerns, but help you realize that they – these mighty warriors of the academic world – are human beings with whom you can have sensible and intelligent conversations, and who may also provide you with unexpected advice that helps the article better fit the journal's requirements.

Deciding when to send your article to a journal

Now it may be very tempting to send your article in when you feel really pleased with it. After all, once a first full draft is complete, the really hard bit of structuring your argument is also complete. You've provided the initial 'hook' for the reader: you've demonstrated strong knowledge of the literature, you've shown how your article contributes to the corpus of knowledge; you've presented your research interestingly and rigorously; you've drawn out the implications of what has been argued through the conclusions, and you've done this in a well-structured and clearly expressed manner. So you're ready to send it off, yes?

Well, no. To achieve a quality piece of writing, you almost certainly still need to amend it, to add some bits, delete others and to re-polish the whole thing. So there will likely be another draft before it's ready, and probably another after that. And be honest with yourself: if you read a draft and recognize that some parts are not covered well enough, then you can be sure that experienced journal referees will see this as well. You've then got more homework to do. And if you don't do this, you're really lowering the chances of the article being published.

So you do all of this, you've gone through the drafts, you've done as many changes as you think are necessary, and you're as happy with it as you think you can be. So you're ready to send it off, yes?

Well, sadly, no, again. Some really good advice, which works well for aspiring academic writers, comes, perhaps a little surprisingly, from the horror writer Stephen King (2000). In his book *On Writing*, he suggests that once you're satisfied with what you've written, you should leave it for a few days until you've forgotten its details, and then read it again with fresh eyes. You'll then almost certainly see issues you hadn't spotted before, and the editing you do now will make the paper that much better.

But King suggests that it's still not ready to be sent to a journal, but instead should now go to friends and colleagues. We suggest that you to send it, if possible, to people with different talents:

The first is *the intelligent non-expert* – the person who will look at your work and say 'I haven't got a clue what you're talking about here ... there are far too many acronyms ... this sentence is far too long ...' or 'you've made it really interesting ... your writing really flows ... .' They are the kind of person who makes comments about the readability of the paper (and implicitly, then, about its structure).

The second kind is *the generalist in your area* – the person who knows your academic discipline, but isn't really an expert in it; but they will be able to make links to other areas within the discipline (and perhaps beyond), and ask questions about those links. In so doing, they will probably widen and enrich the paper.

The final kind is *the specialist in your area* – the person who works in the same area as yourself, and is therefore able to make deeper and more incisive comments about the literature you quote, and your analysis and conclusions, because they know the literature and research surrounding it.

We've developed over the years an unspoken agreement to read each other's papers when requested, and we have similar agreements with other people who fit the different categories above – with the agreement to read *their* materials when they send them to us. We then have gradually formed overlapping unofficial reading groups – and if some of these are leaders in their fields, then all the better, because they can also provide a view on what standard the paper is likely to reach in any review of its academic quality. It's a good idea then to establish such practices yourself. You'll also probably develop friends for life in the process.

And now that you have delayed so that you can read your paper with fresh eyes, and have got others with different talents to read it as well, and you've made all the changes they suggest with which you agree, then you can send it off – or, if you've got the patience, you may leave it for one last week, and re-read one final time. But that's enough: you could keep adjusting forever, and you have to develop the ability to know when it's ready to go. So now send it in, and await the response.

Dealing with journal feedback

Once upon a time, authors got a letter of feedback; nowadays you're much more likely to get an email. And the feedback essentially boils down to four types:

a It fits the journal well; it is of sufficient quality, and it will be accepted unaltered, or with only minor revisions.

b It fits the journal purposes, but it needs a number of changes or revisions before it is ready for publication.

c It fits the journal's purposes, but it is not of sufficient quality, and therefore is rejected.

d It doesn't fit the journal's purposes, and therefore is rejected.

After the advice already given on selecting the appropriate journal, we assume that your paper will fit journal purposes, so comment will only be made on (a) to (c) above.

You may also think these sound much like the judgements possible for your doctorate, and you wouldn't be far wrong; and like comments on a doctorate, it is the middle range of remarks – those that state that it's pretty good, but needs more work – which provides the most problems of interpretation. However, and uncomfortably for the new journal writer, it's much more usual to be rejected by a journal than it is to fail a doctorate.

So let's begin with *article rejection*. Virtually every academic who has had material published has a story to tell about rejection. A favourite of one of the authors was when he sent off one of his early articles to *The Journal of Applied …* only to find that it was rejected because it was 'too applied'. He sent it on to the *Oxford Review of Education*, where it was accepted with only minor revisions. Sometimes the logic of rejection doesn't seem to make that much sense.

However, even though you are likely to be very disappointed, in nearly all cases, don't bother to fight the judgement. The journal is unlikely to give you constructive feedback (largely because they don't have the time), and if you are going to conduct a post-mortem on its rejection – and it *is* a good idea to do this – then do it with a good and highly informed friend. They need to be a *good* friend because they need to read the article for you, they need to have empathy for your feelings of rejection, and they need to treat you gently but honestly. In addition, they need to be *informed*, because they need to have a skilled opinion on why it was rejected. Such feedback won't mean you get it accepted in the next journal you send it to (duly amended, of course, to its different needs). But you will begin to build a body of tacit knowledge that will help you get published. And as you achieve more acceptances, you'll build up a tacit knowledge of why things succeed as well. Little of this will be much comfort at the time of rejection, but you need to be honest in recognizing the things you need to change, and persistence in not giving up. Both of these qualities need strong cultivation.

However, as we said, the *middle ground* is the most problematic. Now, sometimes the feedback on the changes required is straightforward: you are asked to do some relatively small things, and if you do these, the article will be accepted for publication. But beyond that, through to outright rejection, there are many kinds of feedback which are not nearly as simple.

However, before we discuss these, let's not get too gloomy. If you do get feedback, then take it positively. The journal readers think there is a good publishable article in what you have written. So do remember to always read any such feedback very carefully. If it's lengthy (it can be a number of pages long) print off copies and highlight what you see as the significant areas needing attention, so that, as with doctoral corrections, you have a clear list to refer to, rather than a long letter.

And use this list to work out which are the simple and which are the more difficult requests; you may find that doing the easy ones first gives you confidence to later tackle the harder ones. If only four out of twenty corrections are difficult, getting rid of an easy sixteen can feel like a large weight being lifted.

If, even after doing this, you still remain unclear about what they want, show the feedback to informed friends for their thoughts; if *they* are unclear, then go back to the journal editor for further clarification.

This, again, is rather like doctoral changes: if you get problematic feedback on revisions there, then go back to the examiners for oral *and written* clarification, and use this written record in any further discussion. If you can sort out these corrections, and you do what they say, then your article should be accepted, and you'll be in print.

So let's now take a number of problematic feedback issues which occur from time to time, and look at how you'd structure replies:

Contradictory feedback by two referees: If you are certain of this, then summarize the contradictions you see, and ask the editor for advice, using the referees' own words in your description of the contradictions. Any editor worth their position should rule on this and provide greater clarity.

Individual feedback which could be interpreted in a number of ways: Again, summarize the feedback, and the ways in which it could be interpreted, quote the words used and then ask the editor for his/her interpretation of this feedback. Which interpretation do they want?

Feedback from a referee which suggests that they would have written the article differently, and they want you to do this: This, once more, requires the advice of the editor, so state what you think a referee is asking, and what you have intended, and get them to rule on this. If they come down in the referee's favour, then you need to reflect carefully on whether you want to rewrite the article in this manner, or whether you should seek another journal for your paper.

Feedback which is so lengthy and involved that it will mean virtually writing the article again: Well, if you've performed the kind of analysis on feedback suggested above, you should be able to categorize the required changes into four different kinds:

i those changes which will be easy;

ii those changes which will take you a little time;

iii those changes which will take you a lot of time, but which you accept as necessary;

iv those changes which will take a lot of time, and which you think will actually detract from the quality of the article.

All of (i) to (iii) seem very worthwhile, but on category (iv) you need to go into negotiations with the journal editor, where you state what you propose to do, and why you don't propose to do other things. The feedback you get on this will help you decide if this journal is really the home for your work.

One last word here: this 'middle-ground' section may seem to you rather less certain and less positive than other sections, but that's because each problem is unique, and involves potentially unpredictable discussions. But never forget: if you manage to do the corrections requested, you will have an article in print. And crucially, at all times, remain polite and logical, and know where you are prepared to give ground, and where you feel you cannot. Clarity, logic and honey usually work far better than clarity, logic and vinegar.

Finally, don't forget to learn from *the straight acceptance*. While you do undoubtedly learn from your mistakes, you can also learn from your successes. You get both positive and negative feedback from your supervisors on the chapters in your thesis, and you should read both kinds of advice carefully, for they tell you not only what *not* to do next time but also what to do. The same applies to accepted articles: you will get feedback from the journal on these, but you can also get feedback from a knowledgeable friend, or a university output review committee, on what you did right. Avoiding the same mistakes again is a good thing; repeating successful practice is also a pretty good habit to get into.

And that's about it: if you're taking ideas from this final chapter, then you've either gained doctoral success already, or you're probably near to completing your doctorate. And if you've followed the advice given throughout the book, you should have a logic, a structure and an argument to your thesis which will make it very attractive to your external examiners and make it very hard for them to fail it. But we will add one last thing, and one which you've probably realized by now. Your thesis, and the articles that come from it, are the outcomes of a particular period in your life, and a statement of your thinking and research by the end of this period. You may well have decided that the thesis was most valuable in making clear to you what really matters in your research journey, and it is to this that you now want to turn. We wish you well.

REFERENCES

Albuhairi S. (2015) *Preliminary Factors Necessary for Effective Implementation of Cooperative Learning, and Their Prevalence in Cooperative Learning Practice in Saudi Arabia.* Unpublished PhD Thesis, University of Hull, UK.

Alhatlani M. (2018) *Exploring the Perceptions of Informed Individuals about the Education Provisions of Bidoun in Kuwait.* Unpublished PhD Thesis, University of Hull, UK.

ASEAN (2007) ASEAN Qualifications Reference Framework. Available: asean.org/.../ED-02-ASEAN-Qualifications-Reference-Framework-January-2016.pdf.

Ayer A.J. (1940) *Language, Truth and Logic.* Gollancz: London.

Barnbaum D.R. and Byron M. (2001) *Research Ethics: Text and Readings.* Prentice Hall: New Jersey.

Bhaskar R. (1996) *Plato etc: Their the Problems of Philosophy and Resolution.* A 139 word sentence which won the Bad Writing Contest run by the journal *Philosophy and Literature. (THES 15/11/96).*

Bjornavold J. (2013) *Global National Qualifications Framework Inventory.* Available: www.cedefop.europa.eu/files/2211_en.pdf.

Bottery M.P. (1986) *Bases for a Methodology, Content, and Psychology of Moral Mducation.* Unpublished PhD thesis, University of Hull, UK.

Bryman A. (1992) *Quantity and Quality in Social Research.* Routledge: London.

Bryman A. (2015) *Social Research Methods.* 5th Edn. Oxford University Press, Oxford.

Buckles J. (2015) *What are the Educational Implications of Developing a New Social Imaginary, Brought about by the Challenges to be Faced in the 21st Century?* Unpublished EdD thesis, University of Hull, UK.

Carr E.H. (1964) *What Is History?* Penguin Books: Harmondsworth.

Chalmers A.F. (2005) *What Is this Thing Called Science?.* 3rd Edn. Open University Press: Milton Keynes.

Cohen L. and Manion L. (1994) *Research Methods in Education.* 4th Edn. Routledge: London.

Council of Ministers of Education, Canada (2007) *Ministerial Statement on Quality Assurance of Degree Education in Canada.* Available: https://www.cicic.ca/1286/pan_canadian_qualifications_frameworks.canada.

Denzin N. and Lincoln Y. (2000) *Handbook of Qualitative Research*, 2nd Edn. Sage: London.

EQF (2005) *European Qualifications Framework*. Available: https://ec.europa.eu/ploteus/en/content/descriptors-page.

Feyerabend P. (1978) *Against Method*. Verso: London.

Field A. (2005) *Discovering Statistics using SPSS*. Sage: London

Guccione K. and Wellington J. (2017) *Taking Control of Writing Your Thesis*. Bloomsbury: London.

HKQF (2017) *Hong Kong Qualifications Framework*. Available: https://www.hkqf.gov.hk/en/KeyFeatures/levels/index.html.

Israel M. (2014) *Research Ethics and Integrity for Social Scientists*. Sage: London.

Kennett R.J. (2009) *Implications for the Selection and Training of Hostage Negotiators, Through an Analysis of Hostage Negotiation Data*. Unpublished EdD Thesis, University of Hull, UK.

Kerlinger F.N. (1969) *Foundations of Behavioural Research*. Holt, Rinehart & Winston: New York.

King S. (2000) *On Writing: A Memoir of the Craft*. Hodder and Stoughton: London.

Kuhn T.S. (1996) *The Structure of Scientific Revolutions*, 3rd Edn. University of Chicago Press: Chicago, IL.

McQuillan D. (2011) *The Changing Face of the Catholic Voluntary Secondary School in Ireland. The Experience of a Cohort of First Lay Principals*. Unpublished PhD thesis. Dublin City University, Ireland.

Miles M. and Huberman M. (1994) *Qualitative Data Analysis: An Expanded Sourcebook*. 2nd Edn. Sage: Thousand Oaks, CA.

O'Dea M. (2011) *A Framework of Gameplay for the Pedagogical Design of Educational Games*. Unpublished PhD thesis, University of Leeds, UK.

Philips E.M. and Pugh D.S. (2010) *How to get a PhD: A Handbook for Student and Their Supervisors*. McGraw-Hill Open University Press, Maidenhead.

Polanyi M. (1958) *Personal Knowledge: Towards a Post-Critical Philosophy*. Routledge & Kegan Paul: London

Popper K.R. (1982) *The Logic of Scientific Discovery*. Hutchinson: London.

QAA (2014) *The UK Quality Code for Higher Education* Available: www.qaa.ac.uk/en/Publications/Documents/qualifications-frameworks.pdf.

Resnick D.B. (1998) *The Ethics of Science: An Introduction (Philosophical Issues in Science)*. Routledge: New York.

Rittel H.W.J. and Webber M.M. (1973) 'Dilemmas in a general theory of planning', *Policy Sciences*, 4: 155–169.

Rudestam K.E. and Newton R.R. (1992) *Surviving Your Dissertation: A Comprehensive Guide to Content and Process*. Sage: London.

Shotter J. (1975) *Images of Man in Psychological Research*. Methuen: London.

Simane M. (2015) *Czech Minority Primary Education During the First Czechoslovak Republic*. University of Brno: Czech Republic.

Strentz T. (2006) Psychological Aspects of Crisis Negotiation. Published in the USA by CRC Group Taylor and Francis New York.

Wilkinson S. (2017) *The Wicked Problem of Prison Education: What Are the Perceptions of Two Key Stakeholder Groups on the Impact of Tame and Wicked Approaches to Prison Education?* Unpublished EdD thesis, University of Hull: UK.

Wellington J. (2013) 'Searching for "doctorateness"', *Studies in Higher Education*, 38:10, 1490–1503.

Wong Ping-Ho (2005) *A Conceptual Investigation into Spirituality and Conditions for Education in Spirituality, with Application to the Case of Hong Kong*. Unpublished PhD Thesis, University of Hull: UK.

APPENDIX

Some references for grounded theory and action research

Grounded theory

Bryant A. and Charmaz K. (Eds.) (2007) *The SAGE Handbook of Grounded Theory*. Sage Publications: Los Angeles.

Charmaz, Kathy. (2014) *Constructing Grounded Theory*, 2nd Edn. Sage Publications: London.

Clarke, A. (2005) *Situational Analysis: Grounded Theory after the Postmodern Turn*. Sage Publications: Thousand Oaks, CA.

Glaser B. (1992) *Basics of Grounded Theory Analysis*. Sociology Press: Mill Valley, CA.

Glaser B.G. and Strauss A.L. (1967) *The Discovery of Grounded Theory. Strategies for Qualitative Research*. Aldine: Chicago, IL.

Action research

Altrichter H., Posch P. and Somekh B. (1993) *Teachers Investigate Their Work: An Introduction to the Methods of Action Research*. Routledge: London.

Burns, D. 2007. *Systemic Action Research: A Strategy for Whole System Change*. Policy Press: Bristol.

Greenwood, D. J. and Levin, M. (2007) *Introduction to Action Research*, 2nd Edn. Sage Publications: Thousand Oaks, CA.

Noffke S. and Somekh B. (Eds.) (2009) *The Sage Handbook of Educational Action Research*. Sage Publications: London.

INDEX